FUNDING YOUR RESEARCH IN THE HUMANITIES AND SOCIAL SCIENCES

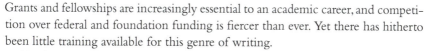

Grants and fellowships are increasingly essential to an academic career, and competition over federal and foundation funding is fiercer than ever. Yet there has hitherto been little training available for this genre of writing.

Funding Your Research in the Humanities and Social Sciences demystifies the process of writing winning grant proposals in the humanities and social sciences. Offering practical guidance, step-by-step instructions, and examples of successful proposals, Walker and Unruh outline the best practices to crack the proposal writing code. They reveal the most common peeves of proposal reviewers and offer advice on how to avoid frequent problem areas in conceptualizing and crafting a research proposal in the humanities and social sciences. Contributions from agency and foundation program officers offer the perspective from the other side of the proposal submission portal, and new research funding trends, including crowdfunding and public scholarship, are also covered.

This book is essential reading for all those involved in preparing funding applications. Graduate students, research administrators, early career faculty members, and tenured professors alike will gain new and effective strategies to write successful applications.

Barbara L. E. Walker is the Director of Research Development for the Social Sciences at the University of California Santa Barbara, USA, where she is also Special Assistant to the Executive Vice Chancellor for Diversity Initiatives. Walker was a founding Board Member of the National Organization of Research Development Professionals (NORDP).

Holly E. Unruh is the Associate Director of the Undergraduate Research Opportunities Center at California State University, Monterey Bay, USA. She previously served as the founding Associate Director of the University of California Institute for Research in the Arts, and Associate Director of the University of California Santa Barbara Interdisciplinary Humanities Center.

FUNDING YOUR RESEARCH IN THE HUMANITIES AND SOCIAL SCIENCES

A Practical Guide to Grant and Fellowship Proposals

Barbara L. E. Walker and Holly E. Unruh

Routledge
Taylor & Francis Group

NEW YORK AND LONDON

First published 2018
by Routledge
711 Third Avenue, New York, NY 10017

and by Routledge
2 Park Square, Milton Park, Abingdon, Oxon, OX14 4RN

Routledge is an imprint of the Taylor & Francis Group, an informa business

Library of Congress Cataloging-in-Publication Data
A catalog record has been requested for this book

ISBN: 978-1-61132-319-1 (hbk)
ISBN: 978-1-61132-320-7 (pbk)
ISBN: 978-1-315-15903-4 (ebk)

Typeset in Bembo
by Apex CoVantage, LLC

CONTENTS

FIGURES

TABLES

BOXES

GLOSSARY OF ACRONYMS

AAUW—American Association of University Women
ACLS—American Council of Learned Societies
AFOSR—Air Force Office of Scientific Research
ARO—Army Research Office
BAA—Broad Agency Announcements
CAREER—National Science Foundation Faculty Early Career Development Grant
CV—Curriculum Vitae
DMP—Data Management Plan
DOD—Department of Defense
DOJ—Department of Justice
DOT—Department of Transportation
ED—Department of Education
FAQ—Frequently Asked Question
F&A—Facilities and Administrative
FOA—Funding Opportunity Announcement
FOIA—Freedom of Information Act
GRFP—National Science Foundation Graduate Research Fellowship Program
HERD—National Science Foundation Higher Education Research and Development Survey
HSS—Humanities and Social Science
ICPSR—Interuniversity Consortium for Political and Social Research
IDC—Indirect Costs
IES—Department of Education Institute for Education Sciences
IRB—Institutional Review Board
K-12—Kindergarten through Twelfth Grade
LOI—Letter of Intent or Letter of Inquiry

NCE—No-Cost Extension

NEA—National Endowment for the Arts

NEH—National Endowment for the Humanities

NIH—National Institutes of Health

MURI—Department of Defense Multidisciplinary University Research Initiative Program

NOAA—National Oceanic and Atmospheric Administration

NSF—National Science Foundation

ONR—Office of Naval Research

PD—Project Director or Program Director

PI—Principal or Project Investigator

PO—Program Officer

PUI—Primarily Undergraduate Institution

R&D—Research and Development

RFP—Request for Proposals

SBE—National Science Foundation Directorate for Social, Behavioral and Economic Sciences

SPO—Sponsored Projects Office

SHTEAM—Science, Humanities, Technology, Engineering, Arts, and Mathematics

STEM—Science, Technology, Engineering, and Mathematics

USDA—United States Department of Agriculture

NOTES ON CONTRIBUTORS

Eve Darian-Smith, Director, International Studies and Professor of Anthropology and Law, University of California Irvine, USA

Susanne Freidberg, Professor of Geography, Dartmouth College, USA

Amy Greenberg, Edwin Erle Sparks Professor of History and Women's Studies, Pennsylvania State University, USA

Bill Maurer, Dean, School of Social Sciences and Professor of Anthropology; Law; and Criminology, Law and Society, University of California Irvine, USA

Joe Meisel, Deputy Provost, Brown University, USA

Stephan Miescher, Associate Professor of History, University of California Santa Barbara, USA

Cora Mirikitani, President and CEO of Asian Americans/Pacific Islanders in Philanthropy. At the time of this writing, she was President and CEO of the Center for Cultural Innovation.

Moira O'Neil, Senior Researcher and Director of Interpretation, FrameWorks Institute, USA

Ann Taves, Professor of Religious Studies and Virgil Cordano OFM Endowed Chair in Catholic Studies, University of California Santa Barbara, USA

Stefanie Walker, Senior Program Officer, Division of Research Programs, National Endowment for the Humanities, USA

ACKNOWLEDGMENTS

Our insights into successful proposal writing have been honed by decades of learning from many amazing colleagues and friends. This book—and indeed our careers—would not have been possible without guidance from, and collaboration with, a series of people and organizations that we would like to gratefully acknowledge.

Two colleagues, in particular, have been instrumental in shaping our approach to proposal writing for the humanities and social sciences: Barbara Herr Harthorn and Karen Lunsford shared their ideas, experiences, and slide decks as we built both our research programs and research development careers at UC Santa Barbara. Their techniques for conceptualizing research ideas and writing introductions were especially crucial in forming our approaches to proposal development. We can't thank them enough for their generosity, collaboration, and friendship.

We also want to express our appreciation for our friends who allowed us to excerpt their excellent proposals and who contributed essays and crucial expertise in this book: Eve Darian-Smith, Aaron Ettenberg, Susanne Freidberg, Amy Greenberg, Bill Maurer, Joe Meisel, Stephan Miescher, Cora Mirikitani, Moira O'Neil, Jai Ranganathan, Ann Taves, and Stefanie Walker.

Many other colleagues at UC Santa Barbara supported the writing of this book in various ways. Our kind bosses and mentors Sarah Fenstermaker, Susan Stonich, Michael Witherell, Melvin Oliver, David Marshall, Dick Hebdige, Kim Yasuda, and Marko Peljhan warmly encouraged us and gave us time to pursue this project. Our many colleagues in the Research Development Office; the UC Institute for Research in the Arts; the Institute for Social, Behavioral, and Economic Research; and the Interdisciplinary Humanities Center have shared their expertise freely, and it has contributed greatly to the collective intelligence that went into this book. We also thank the hundreds of faculty members and graduate students who gave us the privilege of reading and reviewing their proposals over the years. Through workshops, peer review roundtables, and writing groups, the work of proposal writing has been a fantastic medium through which to create caring and inspirational communities of scholars at UC Santa Barbara.

The process of writing and publishing this book was nurtured by our kind and skillful editors, Mitch Allen, Marc Stratton, and Louisa Vahtrick. We thank them for patiently shepherding this project.

The writing of this book largely coincided with the rise of the National Organization for Research Development Professionals (NORDP) and the University of California Research Development Network. We want to acknowledge the importance that members of these organizations have played in creating this book. They have raised the bar and the visibility of the profession and made jobs like ours, and a book like this, viable and valuable in the higher education landscape. We have benefitted professionally and personally, in particular, from our collaborative partnerships and friendships with Susan Carter, Holly Falk-Krzesinski, Alicia Knoedler, Dante Noto, John Crockett, Tim Hushen, Peggy Sundermeyer, Anne Windham, Matt Christian, Jacob Levin, Ann McGuigan, Jacki Resnick, and Jeff Anderson.

Finally, we owe a debt of gratitude to the many funding agencies, program officers, and reviewers who have both rejected and funded our own research proposals over the decades. This has been the formative ground that shaped and improved our understanding of proposal writing and research. Special thanks, of course, goes to those who funded us! They are the City of Santa Barbara Redevelopment Agency, the Elsevier Foundation, the John D. and Catherine T. MacArthur Foundation, Just Communities, the National Oceanic and Atmospheric Administration Sea Grant Program, the National Science Foundation, the Santa Barbara County Arts Commission, the Social Science Research Council, the UC Berkeley Institute for International Studies, UC Mexus, the UC Office of the President, and the U.S. Department of Education. Without exception, the program officers we have worked with over the years have been generous with their time and information, empathetic with our research missions, and supportive from proposal submission to final report and beyond. Working with all of them and the agencies they represent has been a true honor.

BW:

My co-author Holly E. Unruh has been a steadfast comrade through years of exciting projects and initiatives. Working together on this book sealed our friendship and kept us laughing through some astonishingly dynamic years in our lives. Gracias amiga! This book would also not have been possible without my dissertation advisor, Michael Watts, and the brilliant cabal of political ecology graduate students who were my contemporaries at Berkeley. Michael often assigned research proposals as the culminating project in his graduate seminars. He and my fellow graduate students' early guidance in my career fundamentally shaped the art and practice of proposal writing described in this book. Beyond the walls of the Ivory Tower, there is a group of wonderful people who contributed in countless ways to this book: Ken Greenberg, Joaquin Greenberg, Miguel Greenberg, Santiago Greenberg, Lucille Walker, Richard Walker, and Jimmy Walker. Their love means everything to me.

HU:

I am continually inspired by the vision, enthusiasm, and tireless work ethic of my co-author Barbara Walker. Her knowledge and dedication—and humor—have been inspirational since we first met at UC Santa Barbara many years ago. It was through Barbara that I was first introduced to NORDP and began to see that the lessons I had learned administering arts and humanities grant programs could be shared with a wider audience of faculty researchers. Two of my colleagues at the University of California were especially instrumental in shaping my passion for this work: Dick Hebdige, who first hired me as a research development coordinator at the UC Santa Barbara Interdisciplinary Humanities Center and who gave me a great many opportunities throughout the years, and Dante Noto, my very dear colleague and mentor at the UC Office of the President. I also have a few extraordinary people outside of academia that I would like to thank—Tyler Guttenberger, Aiden Unruh-Nichols, Alex Unruh-Nichols, June Gill, and Gary Unruh. Thank you all.

PART I
Prelude to a Proposal

1

INTRODUCTION

Why We Love Research Proposal Writing

Writing grant and fellowship proposals can be some of the most enjoyable writing in your academic career. Even for those of us who loathe writing (yet still haven't made the connection that we perhaps chose the wrong line of work), proposal writing is a breath of fresh air in the suffocating schedule of writing assignments that never ends for academics. Proposal writing is akin to sitting down to compose the annual letter to Santa. It is possibly the most creative writing that we do as academics—some might even call it fiction writing. Where else can you lay out a beautiful, innovative, and elegant research plan uncomplicated by the realities of fieldwork, the drudgery of coding data, and all the other nuisances that make the best laid hypotheses and plans go awry? And let's talk about the payoff! Proposal writing does not end with a piece of work that in its highest glory is read by the twenty other people in your subfield. No, with proposal writing, you can earn cold hard cash. Who isn't motivated by that? There is nothing sweeter in academia than getting the call or the e-mail message from an agency program officer exclaiming: "Congratulations! You have received an award!" Besides getting tenure, not many things in your academic career will make you clap your hands and jump up and down with joy. Receiving a grant or fellowship does that. And proposal writing is the way to get there.

Academic research proposal writing is a unique genre unlike any other type of academic writing that we do. And for many scholars—faculty members and graduate students alike—the process of writing and submitting a proposal is shrouded in mystery. Few departments offer proposal writing courses, and students and junior faculty members don't read proposals on a regular basis as they do journal articles and books. Several excellent proposal writing guidebooks are available (and we list our favorites throughout this book and in Chapter 15), but none of them cater to the academic humanities and social sciences (HSS). Faculty members in HSS in particular do not typically model grantsmanship for students and junior colleagues. In fact, many scholars in our disciplines write proposals secretly, not wanting to admit our ambitions in the humiliating event that our proposal will be rejected. Some of us sidestep rejection altogether by not writing grant proposals at all.

Like it or not, proposal writing and receipt of extramural funding is increasingly expected as part of a successful career in academe. State economies are squeezing higher education budgets, and federal funding for research has been stagnant, at best, for the past decade. The small pots of money for pilot studies or meetings, once available from your department or academic senate, have dwindled. At the same time, standards for landing a faculty job and achieving tenure have escalated at a steady clip. It doesn't matter if you work at a primarily undergraduate institution (PUI) with a heavy teaching load or at a research-intensive university; new emphasis is being placed on grantsmanship and extramural funding across the disciplines. At academic job interviews, deans and department chairs will ask you about your grants and fellowship record. Some departments require an extramural grant for tenure. Colleges and universities are increasingly establishing Offices of Research Development and hiring proposal writing and research strategy experts to help catalyze more and better grants and fellowship activity by individual faculty and teams of researchers. For the majority of graduate students and new faculty members, writing proposals for grants and fellowships is an essential element of your academic career.

Our Target Audience and Terms Explained

Within this milieu of mounting expectations for grantsmanship in the HSS disciplines, within a highly competitive funding environment, this book is designed to help graduate students, post-doctoral scholars, new faculty members, and senior faculty members who have little experience with proposal writing. Our focus is on institutions of higher education/research and funding agencies and foundations in the United States, although much of our advice will also apply to funding opportunities from foreign sources. We understand that some readers of this book may not be affiliated with an institution or may be in a job title that does not make you eligible to apply for academic research grants. Generally speaking, you will need to have an affiliation at an accredited institution to apply for the majority of the grants and fellowships discussed here, although there are a few exceptions. Covering the humanities and social sciences in one book can sometimes be fraught with overgeneralization. However, proposal writing for these disciplines share more commonalities than differences.

As we will emphasize throughout the book, extramurally funded research is not limited to the Carnegie-classified "Research Universities" anymore. Research funding is sought by scholars across the disciplines in all categories of institutions of higher education. In fact, many funding agencies and foundations take measures to ensure that their funding reaches a broad audience, including teaching–intensive and community colleges, where research activities and experiences often have a higher impact on low-income, first-generation, and underrepresented students and faculty members.

In this book we use the terms "grant" and "fellowship" somewhat synonymously; however, there can be important differences between the two and other types of funding that dictate how you apply and how the funds will be administered. These differences are discussed in more detail in Chapter 2. We also alternately use the terms "university," "institution," "college," and "campus" in this book to refer to any institution of higher education and/or research from which you may apply for research funding. This brings us to the term "research" itself. We will frequently use "research" as shorthand for any number of scholarly and creative activities funded by grants and fellowships across the HSS disciplines. Please forgive this oversimplification if you feel that the term does not capture your work.

Why Pursue Funding in the Humanities and Social Sciences?

You've bought this book, so do we really need to convince you? Probably not, but even among the faculty members and students who come to us for help, there are serious misgivings about their motivations for writing grant proposals. Based on conversations that we've had with hundreds of scholars, there are endless reasons why you do not want to write a funding proposal. Here are some of the most common excuses:

> "Funding is not necessary for my research."
> "It takes more time to find funding opportunities and write a proposal than it does to write a journal article, and I don't get any credit in tenure and promotion for proposals."
> "There is no funding out there for humanities and social sciences."
> "They only fund superstars, not me."
> "No one would fund my radical/controversial/cutting-edge/underappreciated research."
> "I hate writing."
> "I don't want to face the pain of rejection."
> "I don't want my colleagues to know I'm a failure."

Under these conditions of high risk for little reward, why should HSS scholars seek research funding?

Although many HSS researchers produce excellent and impactful scholarship with little or no funding, there are multiple ways that research funding can strengthen and enhance HSS research programs, faculty and student experiences, and their academic careers. For individual scholars, even small amounts of funding can provide invaluable benefits, particularly in this age of shrinking university budgets. Grants and fellowships can support various areas of your work:

Materials costs, such as:

- Travel (to fieldwork, archives, libraries)
- Research equipment (a scanner, digital camera, voice recorder, art supplies)
- Routine supplies and expenses for your research (paper, photocopying, telephone services)
- Book subventions and publication costs

Your time away from teaching and campus duties in various ways:

- Course buyout (release time)
- Summer salary
- Long-term residencies at other institutions

Students and research assistance:

- Student research assistant salaries and benefits
- Tuition and fees
- Funds for your students' research

Collaborative and public research:

- Meetings
- Conferences
- Workshops
- K-12 and public outreach and engagement
- Exhibits or productions with museums and theaters

Apart from the research activities and equipment that grants and fellowships can pay for, applying for funding can also benefit your career by increasing the visibility of your research program and scholarly output among your peers. When you submit a proposal for review at an agency, it will likely be reviewed by a panel of experts in your field and those closely related. Even if it is not initially funded, your name and research ideas will be introduced to a new set of scholars and agency personnel through the review process. When your project is funded, the research will be "advertised" on the agency website, as agencies typically highlight their latest awardees through press releases and website features. You may also be included in agency activities such as workshops and conferences. The increased visibility and the circulation of your research can lead to a higher profile in your discipline(s), more citations of your publications, increased contacts and networking within your discipline(s), the potential for new collaborative research activities with other scholars, and higher chances of subsequent funding. Winning grants and fellowships can also contribute to the reputation of your department and university. Many university-ranking organizations account for grants and fellowships in their calculations.

A final benefit of writing grant and fellowship proposals is that it can help you strengthen and sharpen your arguments, scholarly contributions, methods, and overall research program, regardless of whether you get funded. Grant writing improves your research and thinking as you go through the process of methodically and persuasively writing about your project for peer review. Funding agencies will often provide reviewer comments about your proposal, whether or not you are awarded funding. External reviews provide an excellent source of insight and validation of the project, provoking further improvement of your research and scholarship. Thus, the proposal becomes a road map for your work.

Whether your research takes place on a green bean farm in Burkina Faso, in the dim stacks of the Huntington Library Archives, or among environmental activists on the streets of Tokyo, a well-written proposal will come in handy when you begin the act of research itself. Being in the midst of research and fieldwork can be disorienting as the constant inflow of new information tests your assumptions, on the one hand, and numbs the mind on the other. Rest assured, you can always go back to your trusty proposal to see the forest for the trees and refresh your memory about what you said you were going to do in the first place.

Now that you are convinced that you need to compete for research funding and you know what kinds of things you want to fund, it is also important to assess and understand how research and its various forms fit into the arc of your academic career.

Putting Research in Its Place in Your Academic Career

To a large extent, the culture in your discipline, department, or university will dictate the timing of research and research grantsmanship in your career. For both graduate students and junior faculty, this culture (or more formal expectations) for research and research funding are often explained or prescribed by your department chair or advisor. It is always useful to talk with more senior faculty or graduate students in your program as well. Find out when they started submitting grant proposals, what sources of funding they sought, and their experiences with success and failure. Ask your mentors and more senior colleagues if they would be willing to share their research funding proposals—both successful and unsuccessful—so that you can begin to understand the differences between the two.

Sometimes, the patterns of grantsmanship for faculty can be less obvious. This is partly because different people begin their academic careers at different stages. It is increasingly common for junior faculty to begin an assistant professor appointment after a couple of years in a post-doctoral fellowship or as an adjunct professor or lecturer. Many faculty use this time to write or publish their first book or convert their dissertation chapters into published articles. As such, they are coming into their academic career with a different set of research needs and objectives than someone who started their assistant professor position the month after they filed their dissertation (yes, miracles still happen from time to time!).

As a junior faculty member, or even as early as the job interview, have conversations with your department chair, dean, and/or colleagues in your department to find out if such a culture exists at your university. Here are some key questions to ask about the expectations for grantsmanship in your department:

- Even if extramural funding is not necessary for your research, is extramural funding expected for tenure and promotion?
- Is a big and/or prestigious grant expected for tenure and promotion?
- What research funding is available from the university and when?
- Besides funding, what other resources are available on campus to support research, such as assistance with proposal submission, research and proposal development, and grant administration?

Understanding the culture and expectations, whether they are codified or not, is an important first step in mapping out a feasible research agenda. Regardless of whether or not specific patterns in your discipline or department exist, you need to be intentional about making grantsmanship a part of your career, and you need to plan ahead to achieve your research and funding goals. As you begin your career as a graduate student or junior faculty member, think through the next six to seven years of your life, and decide where research funding will be necessary in reaching your goals. For example, as a graduate student you know that you will need funding to do your dissertation research and potentially for writing up the dissertation. If you are doing overseas fieldwork you may require pre-dissertation seed funding to find your optimal research site and meet important field contacts. In your first year or two as a junior faculty member you may need time off from teaching to convert your dissertation into a book. Or you may need seed funding to collect preliminary data for your next big research project. After two or three years, it may be time to bring in a large grant that will allow you to hire research assistants and collect data for your next book or series of research articles.

A variety of research funding in the social sciences and humanities is available to meet different goals at different points in your career. Tables 1.1 to 1.3 chart the different options to consider, depending on your career stage.

TABLE 1.1 Graduate School Research Funding Chronology

Category	Timing of Eligibility	Description	Examples
General Graduate Fellowship	The first several years of graduate school, prior to your dissertation research. Sometimes these grants will include your dissertation research. You may be required to apply for some of these at the time that you are applying to graduate school.	One to multiple years of funding for tuition, fees, and living expenses. A research stipend may be included.	• Multiyear grant from your department or graduate division that might include a combination of teaching assistantships and research assistantships. • National Science Foundation (NSF) Graduate Research Fellowship Program (GRFP) • Ford Foundation Pre-doctoral Fellowship Program
Predissertation Fellowships or Seed Funding	Prior to your dissertation research, while formulating your research design and prospectus.	A couple of weeks to a year of funding for preliminary research and data collection, travel, language training, or methods training.	• Department or university research center seed grant • Social Science Research Council Dissertation Proposal Development Fellowship • Center for Advanced Study in the Visual Arts • National Gallery of Art Pre-doctoral Fellowships for Historians of American Art to Travel Abroad
Dissertation	During your dissertation research	Several months to two years of funding for travel, living expenses while conducting research, research supplies, data analysis software, human subjects payments, stipend or salary for research assistants, transportation in the field (to purchase or	• NSF Doctoral Dissertation Research Improvement Grant • American Association of University Women (AAUW) Dissertation Fellowship

(*Continued*)

TABLE 1.1 (Continued)

Category	Timing of Eligibility	Description	Examples
		rent a car, pay for taxis or bus trips, etc.), conference travel, photocopying, and communications.	• Wenner-Gren Foundation Dissertation Fieldwork Grant
Dissertation Writing	While writing your dissertation	One to multiple years of funding for tuition, fees, and living expenses. If traveling to another institution, access to an office, e-mail address, library, parking, and other campus privileges are typically included.	• Mellon/American Council of Learned Societies (ACLS) Dissertation Completion Fellowship • Graham Foundation Carter Manny Award • Woodrow Wilson Foundation • Charlotte W. Newcombe Doctoral Dissertation Fellowship
Post-Doctoral Fellowship	Post-doctoral years, prior to landing a professor position	One to multiple years of funding for living expenses. A research stipend may be included. Institutional affiliation and access to an office, e-mail address, library, parking, and other campus privileges. Teaching or other academic labor may be required, such as conducting research for a faculty member, teaching courses, planning a conference, administering a grant, etc.	• University of California President's Postdoctoral Fellowship • NSF Directorate for Social, Behavioral and Economic Sciences (SBE) Postdoctoral Research Fellowship • Robert Wood Johnson Foundation Health & Society Scholars

TABLE 1.2 Faculty Research Funding Chronology—Junior Faculty and New Investigator

Category	Timing of Eligibility	Description	Examples
New Investigator, Early Career Award	Pretenure. Thresholds of eligibility vary by agency.	One year to multiple years of funding for various purposes, depending on the funder. Funding could include any combination of the following: course buyout, summer salary, graduate student stipend or salary, graduate student tuition and fees, post-doctoral scholar salary and research support, research and data collection, travel, living expenses while conducting research, research supplies and equipment, technical assistance (subcontracts), data analysis software, human subjects payments, transportation in the field (to purchase or rent a car, pay for taxis or bus trips, etc.), conference travel, photocopying, and communications.	• NSF Faculty Early Career Development (CAREER) Grant • Sloan Foundation Research Fellowship • William T. Grant Scholars Program • American Academy of Arts and Sciences Visiting Scholars Program

TABLE 1.3 Faculty Research Funding Chronology—Junior Faculty, Midcareer, and Senior

Category	Timing of Eligibility	Description	Examples
Seed Grant	Pre- and post-tenure	One or multiple years of funding for small-scale research and related expenses, graduate student assistance, research travel, conference travel, etc. In some disciplines, these funds will cover entire (small) research projects. In other disciplines, these funds might only cover preliminary and pilot data collection.	• Institutional startup funds for new faculty • Institution's academic senate • Institution's social science/humanities/or arts research center • National Institutes of Health (NIH) R21 Exploratory/Developmental Research Grant Award • National Endowment for the Humanities (NEH) Summer Stipends

(*Continued*)

TABLE 1.3 (Continued)

Category	Timing of Eligibility	Description	Examples
Individual, Regular, Investigator-Initiated, Unsolicited Grant	Pre- and post-tenure.	See earlier description under new investigator, early career award.	• NIH Research Grant (R01) or Small Grant (R03) • NEH Fellowship and other grants • National Endowment for the Arts (NEA) Literature Fellowships • Robert Wood Johnson Foundation Investigator Awards in Health Policy Research
Residential, visiting fellowship	Pre- and post-tenure	Several months to two years of funding for salary replacement (assuming that you forego salary at your home institution) while you are in residence at the funding institution. A research stipend may be included. Institutional affiliation and access to an office or studio, e-mail address, library, parking, and other campus (or institute, library, etc.) privileges. Teaching, collaborative work with other scholars, and/or making presentations at colloquia may be required.	**Junior:** • Stanford Center for Advanced Study in the Behavioral Sciences Residential Fellowship • Radcliffe Institute Fellowship Program • Huntington Library Fellowships **Midcareer/Senior:** • Russell Sage Foundation Visiting Scholar Program • ACLS Frederick Burkhardt Residential Fellowships for Recently Tenured Scholars • Rockefeller Bellagio Creative Arts Fellowships • Fulbright U.S. Scholar Program
Training Grants	Pre- and post-tenure	Time periods and scope of funding vary by opportunity. Some programs are small residential short courses on a specific topic. Others are multiyear research and training grants that allow midcareer scholars to retool their skills and expertise and pursue new lines of research.	• Mellon New Directions Fellowship • NSF Cultural Anthropology Methodological Training Scholars Awards • American Association of University Women (AAUW) Career Development Grants

Category	Timing of Eligibility	Description	Examples
Collaborative Research Center and/or Team Science Grants	Associate to full professor. Pre-tenure faculty are not advised to be a lead principal investigator (PI) on a large collaborative grant.	See earlier description under new investigator, early career award.	• NSF Collaborative Research Grants • NSF Science and Technology Centers • NEH Collaborative Grants • ACLS Collaborative Grants
Conference and Seminar Grants	Pre- and post-tenure. However, pre-tenure faculty are not advised to take on the often onerous administrative duties required for conference and seminar planning.	One to two years of funding for planning and conducting a conference, meeting, or seminar series. Funding may include travel, meals, and lodging for participants; rental of meeting space; and administrative or student support for planning the event.	• Mellon Sawyer Seminar Grant • NIH Support for Conferences and Scientific Meetings (R13) • Wenner-Gren Foundation Conference and Workshop Grants
Publication Subvention Grants	Pre- and post-tenure.	Small sums of money ranging from a couple of hundred to a couple of thousand dollars to fund subventions to publish your manuscript, particularly when publication costs are high due to artwork, maps, photographs, etc.	• Association for Asian Studies First Book Subvention Program • American Musicological Society Subventions for Publications Grant • Newberry Library Weiss/Brown Publication Subvention Award
Community-Based Research, Public Scholarship	Associate to full professor. Pre-tenure faculty are not advised to be a lead PI on collaborative grant or to engage in community-based research that may not yield the products that guarantee tenure in your field (such as a book or a series of peer-reviewed research articles).	Time periods and scope of funding vary by opportunity.	• Local foundations and nonprofits in your community • National Oceanic and Atmospheric Administration (NOAA) • The Sociological Initiatives Foundation • National Institute of Food and Agriculture (USDA)

(Continued)

TABLE 1.3 (Continued)

Category	Timing of Eligibility	Description	Examples
Prestigious Senior Fellowships and Awards	Post-tenure and full professor	Time periods and scope of funding vary by opportunity. Some require that scholars be nominated for the award.	• Guggenheim Fellowship • The Templeton Prize

Summary

There are many ways that grants can enrich the research experience for faculty, post-doctoral scholars, and graduate students in HSS. There are multiple benefits from seeking and winning grant funding. There are also a variety of avenues for funding collaborative projects that integrate HSS research with other academic disciplines and community-based projects. This book will walk you through the process of finding the best funding opportunities for your research and career goals. We will explain how to systematically write your grant or fellowship proposal using proven rhetorical and formatting strategies to make your research ideas shine. The book also includes useful explanations about how and when to get funding for collaborative projects and provides many links and references to resources related to effective proposal writing. Finally, we help you make sense of proposal rejection and give you best practices for revising and resubmitting an unsuccessful proposal.

2

FINDING FUNDING

There are many different sources of funding for research and scholarly activities in the humanities and social sciences. The majority of this funding comes from federal and state agencies and private foundations. If you are doing community-based research or public scholarship, you may find additional sources of funding from community organizations and nonprofits, local and state public agencies, and corporate foundations. Crowdfunding is a new and exciting mechanism that many scholars in HSS have engaged to raise funds for their research programs. In this chapter we provide an overview of the recent history of the HSS funding landscape and describe the main sources of funding for HSS research. We also give you tips on how to conduct an effective funding search using both free and subscription web resources. Once you have your target list narrowed down to the most feasible grant and fellowship prospects, we explain how to thoroughly investigate each funder, what they fund, and their review process to make sure that you have found the best fit for your research.

Overview of Recent Trends

The quality of data collected at the national level on funding for academic HSS is uneven, although it is clear that funding for HSS has been stagnant for the last decade. The best measure is the annual National Science Foundation (NSF) Higher Education Research and Development Survey (HERD). Research and development (R&D) is defined as "creative work conducted systematically to increase the stock of knowledge (research) and to use this knowledge to devise new applications (development)" (www.nsf.gov/statistics/srvyherd/). The expenditures reported by institutions include both sponsored research (from federal and foundation sources, for example) and institutional funds (internal grants and fellowships, for example).

NSF began collecting data on non–science, technology, engineering and mathematics (STEM) R&D in 2003, including humanities and visual and performing arts. Social science data have been collected along with science and engineering data since the early 1970s. The data are supplied voluntarily by institutions—typically from offices that oversee accounting, contracts and grants, finances, and/or institutional research. As such, reporting is not uniform (for example, some institutions don't report data for every discipline; history might be in social sciences in one university and humanities in another, etc.), but the NSF has taken recent measures to reduce measurement error to the extent possible. However, these data are considered low-end estimates because of assumed underreporting.

In FY 2015 (the most recent HERD data available), U.S. expenditures for social sciences and humanities were $2.6 billion; under 4% of overall R&D expenditures of $67 billion (see Figure 2.1).

The NSF and the National Endowment for the Humanities (NEH) are the two main federal agencies that fund research and scholarly work in the HSS disciplines. In particular, the NSF Directorate for the Social, Behavioral and Economic Sciences (SBE) had a federal appropriation of $272 million in 2016. The NEH had $148 million.

But federal agencies are by no means the only sources of funding for HSS scholars. For the social sciences in 2015, there was more institutional funding from colleges and universities available than there was from federal sources. For the humanities, you have more than double the chances of receiving funding from your institution than from all other sources combined (see Figure 2.2).

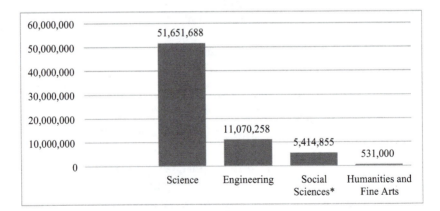

FIGURE 2.1 Higher Education R&D Expenditures by R&D Field: FY 2015 (dollars in thousands)

Source: National Science Foundation, *National Center for Science and Engineering Statistics, Higher Education Research and Development Survey, FY 2015*, www.nsf.gov/statistics/srvyherd/.

* Social sciences includes economics, political science, sociology, business and management, communications, journalism, library science, education, law, social work, and other social sciences (does not include psychology—which is included in science).

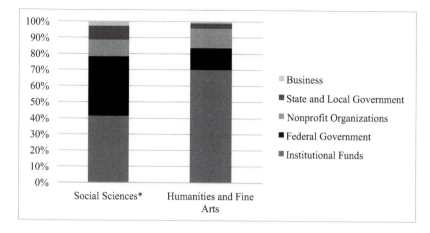

FIGURE 2.2   Higher Education R&D Expenditures by Source of Funds and R&D Field: FY 2015 (dollars in thousands)

Source: National Science Foundation, *National Center for Science and Engineering Statistics, Higher Education Research and Development Survey, FY 2015*, www.nsf.gov/statistics/srvyherd/.

* Social sciences includes economics, political science, sociology, business and management, communications, journalism, library science, education, law, social work, and other social sciences (does not include psychology—which is included in science).

To illustrate a current snapshot of the diversity and amount of funding opportunities available for HSS (as opposed to the earlier data that show actual expenditures by institutions), we did two sample funding searches in one of the leading subscription search engines in winter 2017 (more about these search engines later) (see Figure 2.3). The search yielded 1,621 opportunities for humanities and arts and 3,182 opportunities for the social sciences.

Foundation and nonprofit funding dominates the opportunities available for the humanities and arts, whereas federal funding is almost equal to the funding available from foundations and nonprofits for the social sciences. Availability of funding from academic institutions does not show up as strongly in these data compared to the federal expenditures data earlier because funding available from an institution for its own faculty members and students would not usually be included in a widely used funding search engine.

What do all of these data mean for your funding trajectory? The take-home message is that you cannot be discouraged when your proposal is rejected by the National Endowment for the Humanities or National Science Foundation . . . for the third time in a row. Don't give up on the prestigious federal agencies, but realize that you need to diversify your pool of targets and broaden your funding search to institutional and nonprofit sources to maximize your chances of winning a grant or fellowship. As illustrated by the data earlier, the largest funders of humanities and arts work are private foundations and nonprofit organizations. Although their

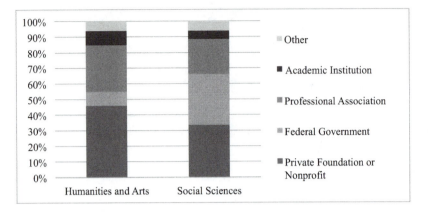

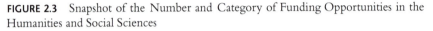

FIGURE 2.3 Snapshot of the Number and Category of Funding Opportunities in the Humanities and Social Sciences

Source: PIVOT, http://pivot.cos.com/.

giving may be more focused on supporting arts and culture institutions—museums and performing arts organizations, for instance—there is also significant giving for scholarly and creative work. Among the largest foundations that fund this type of work are the Andrew W. Mellon Foundation, the Ford Foundation, the Rockefeller Foundation, the Henry Luce Foundation, the Kresge Foundation, and the John D. and Catherine T. MacArthur Foundation. Generally speaking these large foundations can be a good fit for major university requests (programmatic support, major initiatives, long-term goals of the college), or they will funnel their funds through other agencies who then host competitions to fund individual scholars.

Some Key Differences Between Funding Agencies

Before you begin to search for funding, it is useful to know some of the key differences between the different types of funding agencies, particularly federal agencies and foundations. Federal agencies typically have defined grant and fellowship programs with advertised annual or biannual deadlines, and for the most part, these opportunities are stable over time. They may introduce new and/or one-off opportunities from time to time in response to current trends, but it is less common for them to restructure or remove long-standing core funding programs. Because federal agencies are ultimately governed by federal lawmakers, the process of large-scale change in these agencies is slow.

Foundations, on the other hand, are more likely to change their funding priorities and grant mechanisms over time. This can be in response to both current societal trends and the changing desires of the foundation president or board. Additionally, many foundations have less defined submission processes. For example, most federal agencies advertise their funding opportunities through a request for proposals (RFP) (or similar, such as a funding opportunity announcement [FOA] or broad agency announcement [BAA]) that provides program and proposal submission guidance in great detail. Although many foundations have publicly advertised RFPs, they will also often request a brief letter of intent (LOI) before inviting a full proposal.

Federal agencies are more likely to accept proposals in any area of science or scholarship relevant to their agency. For instance, whether you are a scholar of modern food politics in France, or English textuality in 15th-century religious writing, or the art of Aubrey Beardsley, your proposal will receive equal review at the National Endowment for the Humanities. Foundations, in contrast, will only review proposals that are focused on their specific areas of interest. The John Templeton Foundation, for example, currently funds projects on only five topics: science and the big questions, character virtue development, individual freedom and free markets, exceptional cognitive talent and genius, and genetics.

For the most part, grant programs at both federal agencies and private foundations are managed by a program officer (also known as a program director). These individuals are typically well versed in the scholarly field of the program they manage and often have advanced degrees. In fact, many university faculty members do short- or long-term stints as program officers and senior administrators at funding agencies. Program officers at federal agencies manage the review process of proposals, but they do not typically seek or solicit applicants to their programs. At foundations, on the other hand, program officers often identify potential applicants and nurture relationships between the foundation and scholars that can provide expertise in the foundation's areas of interest.

Another key area of difference between federal agencies and private foundations is in the review of proposals. At federal agencies, codified review criteria and procedures are almost always observed. Review panels are composed of peer scholars in the same discipline or field as the proposal writer, and conflicts of interest are not allowed. The merit criteria established by the agency are the most important measures of each proposal. However, some federal agencies may also attempt to ensure a measure of geographic distribution of their awards, as well as distribution across faculty rank or the gender and ethnicity of the applicant. Yet these considerations do not often trump the relative merit of a given proposal. Federal agency program officers do not usually make final award decisions; their job is to manage the review process and submit the judgments of the review panel to senior agency administrators for final determination. This is not to say that federal agency program officers do not have any influence. As respected scholars and experts in their own right, their insights into proposals and their management of review discussions are important in the final ranking of proposals. At the end of the proposal review process, federal agencies provide written review comments and feedback about your proposal, regardless of whether or not your proposal was funded.

At private foundations, on the other hand, review criteria are less defined but are focused on the outcomes of the proposed research on the foundation's mission. The review panel may consist of some scholars in the field of the proposal, but more often consists of foundation board or advisory committee members. Foundation program officers tend to have more authority over grant-making decisions than

TABLE 2.1 Key Differences Between Federal Agencies and Private Foundations

Federal Agency	Foundation
Stable funding programs	Dynamic funding programs
Governed by presidential appointee and federal regulations	Governed by founder and/or board and regulations unique to each individual foundation
Reliable proposal submission deadlines (e.g., RFP)	Less defined deadlines and processes (e.g., LOI)
Will fund any area of science or scholarship relevant to a particular agency	Will fund only projects that meet the foundation mission
Program officer does not find or solicit you	Program officer may find and solicit you
Peer review	Review by board or advisory committee that may not be composed of subject experts
More codified review criteria, more transparent review process	Review criteria less defined, less transparent review process

at federal agencies. And foundations are less likely to provide any feedback about rejected proposals. Of course, there are exceptions. The Mellon Foundation, the American Council of Learned Societies, and the Social Science Research Council, for example, are foundations that focus almost solely on funding academic scholarly activities. Their proposal submission and review processes are very much like those at federal agencies (Table 2.1).

Flavors of Funding and Institutional Policies

Funding for your research and scholarly activities comes in different flavors. The four main categories are:

1. Grants
2. Fellowships
3. Contracts
4. Gifts

When it comes to seeking funding sources and writing your research proposals, you probably won't be too picky about the flavor of money that you're applying for. For the majority of scholars in the humanities and social sciences, any money is good money! The majority of funding for your scholarly work will come from grants and fellowships, with fewer opportunities for gifts and contracts. However, the type of funding that you receive may determine the way that you seek, apply for, spend, and report on your research funds. Typically, these categories are defined in your institution's governing policies, and the administration of each category of funding is circumscribed by institutional, state, and/or federal regulations. Federal funding to educational institutions is governed by the federal Office of Management and Budget in the Code of Federal Regulations. No universal regulations guide foundations and nonprofits in their funding to educational institutions. Be aware that although a particular foundation or agency might call something a fellowship, your institution might define it as a grant, or vice versa. Refer to your Office of Research or Sponsored Projects for your institution's specific policies and guidelines. A general description of each category is follows.

Grant

Grant proposals are submitted by your institution on your behalf, and you will work with your institution to prepare and submit your proposal, which will likely be subject to an institutional compliance review process. Grants obligate an investigator to pursue the research or scholarly activity described in the proposal, which closely follows a timeline and itemized budget, along with other binding terms and conditions. The funding is administered by your institution, and all expenditures must be accounted for. In other words, keep your receipts if you want to be reimbursed for grant expenses. Annual and/or final reporting is required for both the research progress and budget. With most grants, you will need to budget for indirect costs (otherwise known as IDC, overhead, or facilities and administrative [F&A] costs). Chapter 10 describes indirect costs and budgets in more detail. Any unexpended funds remaining at the end of the grant term are returned to the funder. The majority of (but not all) federal funding falls under the grant category, and many foundations also give grants.

Fellowship

Fellowships are often submitted by you as an individual and do not always need to be submitted in coordination with your institution. However, there are many cases when you will want your institution to administer your fellowship funds, so it is always a good idea to be in communication with your Department or Office of Sponsored Projects when submitting a fellowship proposal. Whereas grant funding corresponds to a circumscribed project and budget, fellowship funding is less rigid in its scope. You usually do not submit an itemized budget, as fellowships often come with a one-size-fits-all sum, sometimes on a sliding scale depending on where you are in your career. The funds are generally not tied to individual categories such as salary and equipment, and reporting requirements are less detailed than for grants. Fellowships do not usually require or allow budgeting for indirect costs. Different fellowships pay for different types of things, such as salary replacement, research travel and funding, and/or other expenses necessary to carry out your scholarly activity.

For graduate students, the agency will typically dictate whether the fellowship funding is administered through your institution or if they send a lump-sum check directly to you. Faculty members often have a choice in how their fellowship funding is administered. If a faculty member chooses to receive a lump-sum payment, they will often be required to take an unpaid leave of absence from their institution during the fellowship period. They will also be responsible for the taxes on the fellowship. Many institutions have policies to accept fellowships on behalf of a faculty member in exchange for a period of course release and leave from other duties. Some institutions also have fellowship supplement policies whereby they will "top off" fellowships to match the faculty member's current salary and benefits, sometimes in exchange for sabbatical credits. The majority of fellowships come from foundations and other nonprofit scholarly organizations, such as the American Council of Learned Societies (ACLS). However, some federal agencies, such as the National Endowment for the Humanities, also give fellowships.

Contract

Contracts are similar to grants, in that they are submitted in response to an RFP or similar and will be submitted and administered by your institution. The main difference is that contracts are used by agencies as a means of fulfilling specific program objectives, and the scope and results of the work are stipulated by the agency. Thus, a contract would only work for you if your research is already closely aligned with an agency's, foundation's, or company's mission or if you can provide, for example, a specific type of method, analysis, or evaluation. There is a fixed timeline and schedule of deliverables, and indirect costs apply. Be sure to understand your institution's academic personnel policies related to contract and consulting work. Some faculty members who routinely work on contracts establish their own company or consulting firm, external to their work as a faculty member.

Gift

A research gift is a noncompetitive charitable contribution by a donor to your institution, given specifically to fund your scholarly activities and research. Gifts do not require contractual agreements on how the funding is spent, and the donor does not expect anything in return, other than recognition of the gift in accordance with institutional policies. As you search for funding opportunities, you are not likely to come across any RFPs for gifts. Gifts usually come about as a result of personal connections (with rich people) or when a donor initiates the gift because they have independently discovered your research or scholarly activity and feel passionate about contributing money to it. In some cases, your institution's Office of Development or Institutional Advancement may be involved in identifying a donor for your research. However, funding for individual scholarly activity is generally not the focus of these offices. Yet if you are lucky enough to receive a gift for your research, the funds will need to be routed through your campus Office of Development or Institutional Advancement and may be subject to a gift tax. Indirect costs will not apply. Having said that, it does not hurt to meet with your campus development officer from time to time to keep her current on your exciting research projects and discoveries. You never know when the Development Office might come across a donor who wants to fund exactly what you are doing.

How to Conduct a Funding Search

Now you are ready to do a funding search. The search strategies that we describe here will largely turn up grants and fellowships. Opportunities for contracts and gifts are not frequently posted in funding search engines for academic research. They are typically reached through different channels that often involve personal relationships between you and a contractor or donor. As such, this following information on funding searches will not include how to locate a company that wants to contract your services or how to identify a rich patron who wants to gift your research with a princely sum.

Many free and subscription-based electronic funding search engines are out there. But before you begin your search, it is worth assessing who funds the work of your peers and colleagues in your department or discipline. This is an excellent gauge of which agencies would fund your research as well. When reading journal articles and books in your field, notice in the acknowledgments if a funding agency or foundation is mentioned. Ask your department chair and colleagues who has funded them lately. Check out your colleagues' curricula vitae (CVs) if they are posted on your departmental (or other departments in your discipline) website. This kind of informal search will likely turn up a short list of the usual suspects that routinely fund research and scholarly activity in your area. It will also give you insights into the funding culture of your department or discipline, allowing you to see the funding record that is typical or necessary for producing scholarly work and achieving tenure and promotion.

At the beginning stages of a funding search, you should be open to any and every opportunity that might fund your research. Taking a broad view can help you understand more precisely where your research fits into the current funding landscape. It will also allow you to see how different types of funding and different agencies might support different aspects or stages of your research. It can also help you think about the ways that small or medium-sized tweaks to your research project can lead to more and different funding opportunities. Finally, this broad view might make you realize that your research is simply not of interest to many funding agencies, but it will point you in the direction of the types of research that are currently more in favor. This is not to say that you should abandon your research and go with what is currently popular. We will talk more about thinking through this particular problem in Chapter 5.

The goal at this point is to come to a short list of between five and twenty feasible targets. To get here, we recommend carefully assessing between 50 and 300 funding opportunity abstracts in your search. It is useful to begin putting grant and fellowship information into a spreadsheet to help you sort and make sense of a great deal of information regarding deadlines, funding amounts, agency URLs, applicability to your research goals, etc.

BOX 2.1 FLASH TOPIC: CROWDFUNDING

Within the context of finding gifts to fund your research, consider the possibilities of crowdfunding. Crowdfunding has become increasingly popular in higher education to fund research and other scholarly activities. In short, it works like this:

1. You post information about your project online (known as a "campaign") for a short period.
2. You offer rewards and incentives to potential donors.
3. The public becomes interested and individuals give small to medium-sized donations to your project.
4. You end up with thousands of dollars to carry out your project.

Here are some tips to get you started in this exciting new arena.

Identify the Best Crowdfunding Platform for Your Project

The crowdfunding space is exploding, with dozens of new platforms arriving on the scene every month. You have several hundred options to choose from. How to decide? Much like choosing the right funding agency for your project, you must do your homework on crowdfunding platforms to discover which one is the best fit for you and your project. Start looking online at different platforms and study the campaigns. Look for platforms that host campaigns for academic research and activities. Peruse past and current campaigns to get a sense of how much money they were able to raise and what they look like.

There are several old standbys that host all kinds of campaigns, such as Kickstarter, Indiegogo, and Rockethub. Many of these are well known for hosting academic humanities, arts, and social science campaigns. There are also many new platforms focused specifically on scientific research, such as Microyza, Petridish, Fundageek, and Experiment, and these might also be relevant for other kinds of academic research in the social sciences and humanities.

Once you find a set of potential platforms, dig in deeper to understand their policies. Make sure you understand the terms related to:

- **Pricing Structure and Commissions:** Most platforms will take a cut of the funds that you raise, usually less than 10%. Some require a monthly subscription payment to host your campaign. Some charge processing fees on each payment to your campaign. Related to the next point, some platforms charge different commissions depending on if you reach your goal or not.

- **All or Nothing vs. Take It All:** Some platforms will only fund you if you reach your funding goal, whereas others will fund you no matter how much (or little) money you raise.
- **Transferring Funds to You:** Especially relevant to academics, find out how the platform will deliver the funds. Will they only disburse a check to you (which means that you are liable for the taxes on these funds as personal income)? Or will they cut the check to your university, in which case the funds come to you as a gift through your institution's development or institutional advancement office?
- **Charitable Donations:** Does your donor's contribution qualify as a charitable donation if they are technically donating to the platform, which may or may not be a nonprofit organization? If their donation does not count as a tax write-off, will they still want to give to your campaign?

Understand Your Institution's Policies on Crowdfunding

As crowdfunding has taken off in higher education, colleges and universities are beginning to catch on with policies, guidelines, and sometimes in-house platforms for their researchers. As this is new terrain for higher education, there is often uncertainty at campuses about what crowdfunding is, how it intersects with traditional extramural funding for research, and what the value is for researchers and institutions.

If your campus has a home-grown or contracted crowdfunding platform, find out how you can post your campaign. In some cases, universities will only post a certain number of campaigns at a time, and there may be a waiting list or review process before yours can be posted. Will your campus allow you to post your campaign on an external platform, or are you obligated to use the university's platform?

If you opt for a public platform, does the university have policies about your participation in crowdfunding? Are you allowed to advertise your affiliation with your university in your campaign? What are your institution's policies about accepting gift funds for research? How do campus research compliance policies (human and animal subjects, export control, intellectual property, conflict of interest, peer review, for example) intersect with gift money?

Most institutions are just beginning to think about these issues, and there are no standard practices across higher education. You may be the person on your campus to get this conversation started. Our advice is to do your due diligence with your institution before launching your campaign.

Build It and They Might Come: How to Take Your Project to the Masses

On the face of it, crowdfunding seems too good to be true. Put some scintillating paragraphs about your brilliant research online; throw in an iPhone video of you passionately talking about your research over a stream of compelling images; promise to send doodads and acknowledge each donor in your next book; and voila!: $10,000 to fund your project!

This is indeed the basic recipe for a successful crowdfunding campaign, but posting the campaign on the Web is only the first step. The leading crowdfunding platforms host thousands of campaigns at a time. Very few people take it upon themselves to regularly go to these websites and donate money. Even if they did, yours would not necessarily stand out unless it was chosen as the "Project of the Day" on the home page.

Succeeding with crowdfunding is a lot of work. As the word "campaign" implies, you are responsible for relentlessly advertising, showcasing, and spreading the word about your project far and wide during the weeks or months that your campaign is live. One of the authors of this book, Barbara Walker, has in fact conducted collaborative research on crowdfunding. This research illustrates that *developing a "fan base" for your project is the most important factor in campaign success* (see Byrnes, Ranganathan, Walker, & Faulkes 2014). According to the study, connecting with a large audience through outlets such as Facebook, Twitter, and YouTube is correlated with increased levels of funding.

This means that before you begin to develop your campaign, you need to develop the fan base. If you decide to create a Facebook account or academic blog the same day your campaign launches, that is too late. You want to have hundreds, if not thousands, of social media connections beforehand. This may sound daunting, and if that is the case, then crowdfunding is not for you. But if you are interested in developing more crowdfunding opportunities for your research, a couple of excellent resources are available to help you. The #SciFund Challenge, in particular, is dedicated to the dual mission of science outreach and science crowdfunding. They host a variety of courses through #SciFund University that teach you, for example, how to create an academic blog or a compelling video about your research (http://scifundchallenge.org/). The lessons are universal to all academic disciplines, including social sciences and humanities. Crowdsourcing.org has several posts on crowdfunding components, such as "How to Make a Great Crowdfunding Video for Beginners" and "Five Tips for Designing the Ultimate Crowdfunding Campaign Page Experience" (www.crowdsourcing.org/).

As the crowdfunding trend ages into becoming a standard practice at colleges and universities, make sure to stay tuned for new developments. More platforms and resources are popping up online every day, and you should make time to familiarize yourself with the dynamic world of crowdfunding before launching your first campaign.

Bibliography

Byrnes, J. E., Ranganathan, J., Walker, B. L., & Faulkes, Z. (2014). To crowdfund research, scientists must build an audience for their work. *PLoS ONE, 9*(12), e110329.

"Crowdfunding and the Arts: UCIRA Interviews Thuy Tran of United States Artists (USA), Steve Lambert, Jeff Crouse and Dan Froot (UCLA).", SOTA (October 2011), (http://ucsota.wordpress.com/2011/10/20/crowd-funding-and-the-arts-ucira-interviews-thuy-tran-of-united-states-art-ists-usa-steve-lambert-jeff-crouse-and-dan-froot-ucla-part-1/)

Free Resources

Grants.gov

The federal government has done us all a favor by systematically posting every federal grant opportunity online at www.grants.gov/. It centralizes information on over 1,000 grant programs and provides access to approximately $500 billion in annual awards. Grants.gov has an Advanced Search page that allows you to narrow your search by the amount of time before deadline, applicant eligibility, funding activity category, federal agency, and funding instrument type (such as a grant, a cooperative agreement, a procurement contract, etc.). For the type of funding that you are likely seeking, you will want to narrow in on specific types of opportunities using the Advanced Search page. Specifically:

- Narrow the Eligibility field to "Individuals" and/or "Private institutions of higher education" or "Public and state controlled institutions of higher education."
- In the Category field, choose the most appropriate among "Education" (which may yield fellowship opportunities for students), "Humanities," or "Science and Development and other Research and Development." This latter category is as close as you can get to designating "social science."
- Leave the Agency field open unless you already know that you have specific parameters in these areas.

The Grants.gov search engine also allows you to search for closed or archived opportunities. Be aware that many federal agencies do not publish their RFPs until as little as four weeks before the proposal deadline. Four weeks is not usually enough time to develop and submit a proposal. However, as mentioned earlier, many federal agencies have recurring annual or semiannual deadlines, with small or no changes to the RFPs. Therefore, if you come across a great prospect with a deadline that has passed or is only weeks away, save the information, and start thinking about developing the proposal for next year's deadline. Once you have tried a couple of searches in Grants.gov and are retrieving funding opportunities that reasonably match your criteria, you can subscribe to receive notices by e-mail about any new opportunities that are posted that match your Advanced Search fields.

Many federal funding agencies also have their own internal databases that allow researchers to search for funding opportunities, as well as funding alert subscriptions. The individual agency websites are where you will find more information about past and future opportunities, as well as more detail about the funding opportunity, the names and contact information for program officers, and the broader program context in which a given grant opportunity is embedded.

Foundation Center

Although federal funding opportunity information is readily available through Grants.gov, it is more difficult to find a free aggregator of foundation and nonprofit funding opportunities as well as state- and university-based funding. One excellent place to start though is the Foundation Center (http://foundationcenter.org/). A host of information and services are available from this site for a subscription fee, starting at about $100 per year (discussed in more detail later), but there are several great free resources as well. First, you might consider subscribing to the Foundation Center RFP Bulletin here: http://foundationcenter.org/pnd/info/subscribe.jhtml. They send a weekly e-mail that lists new foundation RFPs with deadlines more than a month away. Categories include Arts and Culture, Education, and Science and Technology, among others. We find the RFP Bulletin particularly helpful for arts and humanities opportunities, but less so for the social sciences. The listings consist only of opportunities that have been submitted by the foundations themselves, so this is not an exhaustive source. Another useful free resource on the Foundation Center site is access to copies of foundation 990-PF tax return forms. If you already know about a particular foundation that funds research in your area, the 990-PF form lists all the foundation's grantees and the amount that was given to each in a given tax year. Knowing this information will help you to assess whether or not your research project fits into the milieu of what they fund and what would be a reasonable amount of funding to ask for. To access these forms on Foundation Center, look for the Find Funder tab on the home page, and click on "990 Finder."

Funding Search Resources for Sale

Several online and print resources are available to grant seekers for a fee. It is likely that your institution has purchased or subscribed to some of these. If not your university, local libraries and nonprofit service centers will sometimes carry subscriptions to online resources and give free access to funding databases. Libraries, both on campus and off, may also have print grant directories on their shelves. Several authors and companies publish a variety of directories on different categories of grants. These include the following.

Humanities

- *Grant Guides* (various topics). New York: Foundation Center. (http://marketplace.foundationcenter.org/Publications/Digital-Grant-Guides).
- *Foundation Grants for Individuals.* New York: Foundation Center (http://marketplace.foundationcenter.org/Publications/Directories).

- *National Directory of Corporate Giving.* New York: Foundation Center (http://marketplace.foundationcenter.org/Publications/Directories).
- *Directory of Grants in the Humanities.* Nashville, IN: Schoolhouse Partners. (Annual publication). (www.schoolhousepartners.net/).

Social Science and General Research

- Schlachter, Gail A. & R. David Weber. *Money for Graduate Students in the Social and Behavioral Sciences.* Los Altos, CA: Reference Service Press (updated regularly). (www.rspfunding.com/index.html).
- *Directory of Research Grants.* Nashville, IN: Schoolhouse Partners (annual publication). (www.schoolhousepartners.net/).
- GrantsWire provides a weekly e-mail listing of recently released funding opportunities. (www.thompson.com/public/offerpage.jsp?prod=GEMS).

These resources are costly, ranging from $40 to over $300, and searching through them is time consuming compared to using an online search engine. A better bet is to find access to one of several leading online grant search engines. Several new companies have entered this market over the last few years, and the pool of search engines to choose from is growing. Check with your campus Office of Research or library if you are not already aware of your institution's subscription service(s). These search engines track tens of thousands of funding opportunities from a variety of sponsors, including federal and state agencies, foundations, non-profits, and universities. The following is a list of the current leading subscription search engines in alphabetical order:

- GrantForward: www.grantforward.com/index
- GrantSelect: www.grantselect.com/
- Grant Advisor Plus: www.grantadvisor.com/
- Grant Domain: www.tgci.com/grantdomain.shtml
- InfoEd SPIN: http://infoedglobal.com/solutions/grants-contracts/spin-funding-opportunities/
- PIVOT: http://pivot.cos.com/
- ResearchResearch: www.researchresearch.com/
- SciVal Funding: www.funding.scival.com

Three subscription databases focus on foundation funding only, covering a great deal of information about what foundations fund beyond their grants that result from RFPs. They are:

- Foundation Directory Online: http://fconline.foundationcenter.org/
- Foundation Grants to Individuals Online: http://foundationcenter.org/findfunders/fundingsources/gtio.html
- Foundation Search: www.foundationsearch.com/

Find out which search engine your campus subscribes to and start using it. If your campus does not subscribe to any of these databases, you may consider subscribing to one as an individual. GrantForward, GrantSelect, Grant Advisor Plus, Grant Domain, and Foundation Grants to Individuals Online have individual subscription rates.

Tips for Effectively Using Funding Search Engines

1. Take the time to watch the online tutorials that are included on the search engine websites. Your campus Office of Research Development or Sponsored Projects may also schedule trainings for faculty and students.
2. Use the "Advanced Search" (or comparable) option, which will give you better accuracy and resolution in finding the most appropriate opportunities. For example, you will be able to narrow your search to "Prize or Award" for "Graduate Students" or "Meeting or Conference or Seminar" for "New Faculty/Investigators."
3. When you get started on a new search, do several searches with different combinations of criteria until you find the combination that gives you a reasonable number of results (reasonable depends on how many abstracts you are willing to read, but we recommend between 50 and 300).
4. Most search engines have embedded keyword typologies by which the company has categorized funding opportunities. Get to know this typology by looking through all the nested categories of keywords available.
5. Also try searching with your own keywords, as some search engines will allow a search through all abstract or RFP language.
6. If you are working on more than one project, do a different search for each—for example, one search for your research project, one search for book subventions, one search for a conference, etc.
7. If your search engine includes an alerting function, use it. You can save your search criteria for any given search, and the system will perform the search every week or so and send you the updated results. You can also set an alert for specific individual opportunities with recurring deadlines if you want to be notified when the next deadline is announced.

Scholar Expertise Databases

Several of the leading search engines are associated with "profiles" or "expertise" databases. These include data about scholars (faculty, post-docs, and students) via publicly available departmental websites, funded grant listings, and/or publication data. The search engines have proprietary algorithms that use your profile data to match you with funding opportunities as well as potential collaborators (or competitors, depending on how you look at it). It is important that you take the time to "claim" your profile and update it with the most accurate information beyond what a computer was able to glean from other sources. Although we think that these automated matches are interesting, do not rely on automation to find the best funding opportunities. After all, you are probably looking to fund a new project, not a project that you have already completed and published.

As for the automated collaborator matches, we find that the best collaborations are made between people who have long-standing relationships, or at least relationships that have been mediated by trusted matchmakers, such as your colleagues, mentors, and perhaps funding agency program officers. Collaboration is hard work, and a growing discipline called "science of team science" is finding that intentional team composition and certain combinations of personality types and diversity are beneficial to successful collaborations. We discuss collaboration in more detail in Chapter 12.

Limited Submission

Another factor to be aware of when you search for funding is "limited submission" opportunities. Many agencies limit the number of proposals that they will accept from a single institution. You will not be able to apply for a limited submission grant or fellowship without approval from your campus. Your campus Office of Research Development or Sponsored Projects will typically hold a campus-wide competition to select the most appropriate proposals that go forward to the agency for further review. Limited submissions are identified in most funding search engines.

Patching Together Resources for Your Project

Earlier in this chapter we suggested that you narrow your search for potential funding opportunities to between five and twenty feasible targets. It is important that you include in that number more than just the large federal agencies. Although an NEH fellowship might be exactly the thing you need to undertake your research or finish the book, the fact remains that very few proposals submitted to large federal agencies are successful the first time around; for example, last year the National Endowment for the Humanities funded only 7% of applications for individual research fellowships and 8% of the applications for collaborative project grants.

As a result, it is important to familiarize yourself with institutional opportunities as well as the many smaller grantmakers and their funding priorities in order to strategize how you can submit multiple proposals to fund different parts of your work should the big individual grant not come through.

When we ask our HSS colleagues what they need most in order to accomplish their work, the answers typically include:

- Time off from teaching at various points within the project
- Travel funds to conduct archival research or conduct fieldwork
- Residency at a specific institute or collection where they can dig into original source materials or write the book
- Subvention funds for publishing

Funding for these kinds of activities can be obtained at the local campus level through departmental or research center funds. Explore the opportunities on your campus first. If you don't know where to begin, ask staff at your Office of Research or Sponsored Projects. For humanities in particular, you should also explore opportunities through local community foundations, as well as those offered by state-level agency funders such as your state humanities council, many of which have thriving grant programs.

Summary

This chapter provides an overview of humanities and social science funding trends, types, and search resources. Understanding the various options can help you formulate a diverse funding plan to fit multiple aspects of your research project. Once you have rounded up a selection of potentially fruitful funders, the next step is to carefully assess each agency and competition process to determine the best fit and the best approach for your project. The next chapter will explain how to do just that.

BOX 2.2   FLASH TOPIC: FUNDING FOR ACADEMIC ARTS

Although this books focuses on grantsmanship for the humanities and social sciences, many lessons and insights also apply to faculty and students in the academic arts disciplines, including fine arts, film, music, theater, and dance. If you are in one of these disciplines, we probably don't have to tell you that there is very little funding for scholarship and academic activities in these areas. Nevertheless, in your pursuit of the pots of money that do exist, several important themes should guide your quest:

- **Coordinate multiple funding sources:** divide your project into smaller subcomponents, and seek funding for each individually; realize that the entire project might come to fruition over several years.
- **Think local:** seek funding from local foundations and state arts councils who are more likely than federal agencies and large foundations to invest in arts.
- **Partner with nonprofits:** partner on creative programs with K-12 schools, museums, and other 501(c)(3) organizations in your local area; they have a broader appeal to different types of nonprofit funders than your university.

Apart from these strategies, many of the same rules of thumb for project development and grant writing apply. The following contribution summarizes tips for success:

Ten Keys to Successful Grant Writing for the Arts

By Cora Mirikitani, President and Chief Executive Officer, Center for Cultural Innovation

I have had the great privilege to work in the nonprofit arts and cultural sector my entire career, spanning more than thirty years, both as a private foundation funder and as an arts organization leader, and now at the helm of a hybrid nonprofit that provides both funding and entrepreneurial training to individual artists.

My work as both a grant maker and grant seeker has taught me a lot about what works and what doesn't in the grantor–grantee relationship and how much we still need to do to demystify the process. In that spirit, I'd like to offer the top ten lessons I've learned about successful grant writing:

1. **Do your homework.** For every cause and in every community, there are a growing number of potential funders to support your work, including private foundations (e.g., independent, corporate, and family), community foundations, nonprofit service organizations (funding "intermediaries"), and governmental arts agencies, to name a few. But casting a blind net to all funders is never a good idea. Instead, you should begin by doing some basic research to see who is funding organizations like yours (scanning event programs or annual reports is a simple way to do this), by asking your colleagues in the field, or by using service providers like the Foundation Center to narrow your list of prospects. And given that most institutional funders now have websites, the search for potential funders who are a good fit with your mission and activities is now faster and easier than ever.

2. **Understand the funder's priorities and aspirations.** The vast majority of institutional funders today try to actively disclose their grant-making priorities, programs, and guidelines, often on their websites, as a way to provide greater transparency and accountability to the public. But although you may read a soaring and inspirational program description that speaks to you (e.g., "The ABC Foundation supports exemplary organizations to create high-quality work that enhances the cultural vibrancy for diverse residents in the community"), don't ever assume that their funding is a good fit for you. Study their program guidelines and criteria carefully to understand important questions such as: *What kind of program outcomes, community impacts, or field changes are they ultimately hoping to achieve? What types of organizations are they seeking to work with or are eligible to apply? What types of supporting evidence or review criteria are they using to make funding determinations?* A realistic, up-front assessment of a funder's process, priorities, and intended outcomes will go a long way in determining if they are a fit for you and, ultimately, your success as a grant seeker.

3. **Have a clear and compelling story to tell.** Okay, so you've done your homework and narrowed the list of funders to those who seem to be a good fit. But if this is a competitive grant-making program, you will likely be going head to head with many other grant seekers who are also

eligible to apply. How do you make your proposal stand out? Over many years of reading literally thousands of grant applications, I have found that the most successful requests are usually the ones with a clear and compelling story to tell—not the longest, most detailed (and sometimes mind-numbing) narratives, but rather those that convey a clear and powerful message about your project/work in alignment with the funder's priorities. One way to test whether your narrative is in the "sweet spot" is to see if you can boil down your essential funding request to an "elevator speech"—a one- or two-sentence statement of who you are, what you are applying for, and why.

4. **Put yourself in the reader's shoes.** Although your grant project may be complex and you and your organization have many accomplishments to speak of, you should also be mindful about who is reading and reviewing your grant request on the other side. If there are peer panel reviewers involved in scoring many grant applications, the reality is that they may spend just five to ten minutes reading your narrative and another three to five minutes reviewing your attachments or work samples. On the other hand, a foundation program officer may be able to devote considerably more time to assessing your grant proposal, which may also include review by other program, administrative, or financial departments in the foundation. So besides having a clear and compelling story, having the right amount of case-making information in your grant proposal to fit the intended reader is an important consideration as well.

5. **Follow instructions exactly.** I know that this seems like an obvious piece of advice, but I can't tell you how often I have seen grant applications that are filled out incorrectly or incompletely, possibly in haste, or instructions or advice from foundation staff in the crafting of proposals that are somehow ignored. Even if it's an honest mistake or omission, in a highly competitive grant-making environment small things like this have the potential to hurt your chances for success.

6. **Present your materials meticulously (especially work samples).** It is always obvious when a grant applicant has spent time to prepare and present a well-designed and well-organized grant proposal or application, starting with no typos, no formatting issues, budgets that add up, and good choices of attachments or work samples. Aside from the important content of your grant request (your project), a meticulous grant application speaks volumes about your high standards and professionalism as a potential grant recipient.

7. **Relationships are important.** I always encourage grant seekers to get to know their funders and to introduce themselves and their work in person, if at all possible, even if it doesn't lead to funding in the short term. This can be accomplished in a variety of simple ways, such as attending

"meet the funder" workshops, serving on grant-funding panels, presenting or volunteering at community events, or even requesting a one-on-one informational meeting with a funder to seek their advice about future funding potential and fit. Building personal relationships is an important long-term strategy if you intend to stay in the nonprofit field—even if you or your funder moves on to new organizations or positions. Good relationships can last forever, and it's never too early to start.

8. **If you do get a grant, do what you said you'd do.** I'm always amazed at the number of grantees who have gotten a highly prized and competitive award and then proceed to drop the ball by ignoring grant reporting requirements and deadlines or, worse than that, failing to deliver what they promised. Sometimes grant-funded projects don't proceed as originally planned, but in either case it's critical that you communicate with your funder in an honest and timely way. Failing to do so will surely harm your chances the next time around.

9. **If you don't get a grant, find out why.** There are always more worthy grant requests to be made than can be funded, even if you're a perfect fit and you've done everything to make your grant request right. But many funders are willing to provide feedback to applicants who are not funded, and you should take advantage of that offer. Use that opportunity to really hear what they have to say and learn from their advice, and by all means, don't take it personally.

10. **Never give up!** Grant seeking is a time-consuming and often discouraging pursuit that can result in many "turndown" letters despite your best efforts. My best advice is to incorporate lessons and tips being learned in the process and to keep applying. The same talent, passion, and single-minded commitment that probably led you to work in the arts are the same attributes that will result in your eventual success as a grant seeker and grantee.

Cora Mirikitani is the President and CEO of Asian Americans/Pacific Islanders in Philanthropy (AAPIP), a national philanthropic membership organization dedicated to mobilizing and expanding resources for underserved AAPI communities and needs. At the time of this writing, she was President and CEO of the Center for Cultural Innovation (CCI), a nonprofit funder and program incubator supporting working artists and creative entrepreneurs in California. Her career in the arts includes more than ten years in philanthropy as Program Officer for Culture at The Pew Charitable Trusts and later as Senior Program Director at The James Irvine Foundation in charge of their Arts program.

3

ASSESSING FUNDING FIT AND FEASIBILITY

Once you have your list of opportunities narrowed down to a reasonable size, it is time to begin researching the funders and their review processes. Even if a particular abstract or RFP seems to have your name written all over it, there is still more research you can do on the agency's website to make sure that the opportunity is a good fit and to find out information that will help you write the strongest proposal possible. To start with, assess what the agency has funded previously in your area. Most funding agencies list their prior awards, and here you can find out helpful information such as:

- Who they have funded (from what discipline, at what institution, etc.)
- Titles of funded projects
- Project abstracts
- Length of award periods
- Amount funded

This information should be weighed in reference to the following types of questions:

- How does your proposed project compare to these?
- Are you planning to conduct a three-year project, but the agency only provides funding for one year?
- How does your ideal budget match up to the amounts they have awarded recently?
- Do the funded project titles or abstracts share common themes and theoretical areas with your project?
- What is the agency's mission? (Be aware that private foundations are more likely to change their funding priorities from time to time. Therefore, abstracts of what they have funded in the past might not match their current grant programs.)

See What Success Looks Like

While you are browsing an agency's list of funded proposal titles or abstracts, look for prior awardees who are your colleagues, acquaintances, or friends and then contact them to politely ask if they would consider sharing their successful proposal with you. Successful proposal writers are typically generous in sharing their proposals with trusted colleagues and acquaintances. Always assure them that you will not share it with others (and then don't share it). If you don't know anyone who has received the grant or fellowship that you are seeking, ask your campus Research Development office. They often keep libraries of successful proposals, or they can find out if anyone on your campus has received the grant or fellowship. If not on your campus, they might contact other Research Development offices in their state or national networks to locate a successful proposal at another institution.

Some agencies, such as the National Endowment for the Humanities, the National Institutes of Health, and the William T. Grant Foundation, have posted successful proposals on their websites. For graduate students, we have seen the recent rise of blogs devoted to particular grants, such as the NSF Doctoral Dissertation Improvement Grant or the Graduate Research Fellowship program. We encourage you to try an Internet search, and you may well find a trove of successful proposals archived on someone's website. For federal grants it is possible to submit a Freedom of Information Act (FOIA) request to acquire successful proposals. All federal agencies are required to make requested records available, including funded grant proposals, unless the records are protected from disclosure by an exemption or exclusion of the FOIA. Each agency has its own guidelines for FOIA requests, but generally speaking, you will need to send a letter to the agency making the request, and sometimes you will be charged a fee. We do not consider a FOIA request to be a good option for accessing successful proposals. We have found that this causes more harm than good for your reputation, because the successful proposal author will know who you are and will wonder why you want their proposal. Even if you receive a successful proposal through this route, it will likely be heavily redacted.

A sample successful proposal makes for an excellent template on which to base your own. Of course we don't mean that you should plagiarize their language or ideas. But you should study funded proposals to gauge:

- How are the research questions or objectives framed in reference to the existing literature?
- How have they divided the proposal into sections?
- Do they use section headers based on RFP guidance? If not, what section headers do they use?
- How much space is devoted to each section of the proposal?
- Do they cite references?
- How often do they cite other work and in which sections?
- How much depth, breadth, and/or detail do they put in the theoretical review, the methods section, the timeline, etc.?
- Do they use any special formatting, such as bullets or boldface, to emphasize important points?

- Do they use infographic devices to help convey complex ideas or processes? How much space do they devote to these?
- How long is their bibliography?
- Have they appended their data collection instrument such as survey or interview questions?
- What is in their budget, and what ratios are allocated to the different categories?

A sample of only one or two successful proposals will not give you absolute clarity on how to write a grant proposal. But if you are a novice proposal writer or have been unsuccessful in winning grants, successful proposals are immensely helpful in guiding the way and answering a lot of basic questions that you might have.

Assessing the Feasibility of Your Project

Proposal writing can put you in a dreamy mode of thinking and writing where your creative juices start to flow, you begin to believe that you are a genius after all, as you visualize research fantasies that involve potentially far-fetched scenarios, such as winning a half-million-dollar dissertation fellowship from a humanities foundation for your brilliant project that requires travel to twenty different foreign archives over three years. Or perhaps it is your amazingly innovative data collection method in which you bring together members of all the Central American drug cartels for a focus group interview. Or maybe it involves procuring a research permit from a country on the State Department Travel Warning list to study their government's human rights violations. Genius? Possibly. Feasible? No!

Although we like to advocate for proposal writing as creative and fun, we also need to put the brakes on your imagination by asking you to think through this outlandish question: What if you get the grant? Because if you do, then you actually have to do all the things you said you would in the proposal. And the fact is that if you propose something a little too implausible, you won't get the funding anyway. So make sure that you do enough research beforehand to determine that you can access the data you'd like to collect, that the informants you need to interview will actually speak to you, that the security classified archives will be released, and that the budget for your project is in line with the amount that you can reasonably expect to get from an agency.

What Are the Odds?

Another consideration when assessing the best funding fit for your research is the success rate for a particular grant or fellowship. This number is not always available and will change slightly from year to year. For the most part, success rates are low. Program officers at the National Science Foundation often quip that you need to "walk on water" or "raise the dead" to get a proposal funded these days. This is because in 2015 at the National Science Foundation, your chances of success were around 24%. At the National Institutes of Health, it was 21%. And for the National

Endowment for the Humanities, the chances of winning the coveted fellowships have hovered around a lowly 7% for the past several years.

Several foundations also publish their funding statistics. For example, the Guggenheim Foundation receives between 3,500 and 4,000 fellowship applications annually, and only about 5% are funded each year. The American Council of Learned Societies makes awards to about 7% of their applicants across all of their fellowships. In general, as you can see, success rates are depressingly low. These statistics are discouraging, but don't be intimidated! Instead, use this information to:

- Determine at which agencies your proposal will have better odds of success.
- Put your failure in perspective if your proposal has been declined; agencies simply can't fund all the great proposals that they receive in a given year. And thus, it is worthwhile to revise and resubmit. At many agencies, resubmissions have a higher rate of success. We give more advice about dealing with failure and resubmissions in Chapter 14.
- Realize that if you want to achieve grant and fellowship success, your proposal needs to be excellent and not merely good.

Understand the Review Process

Another important part of the puzzle to glean from agency websites is information about the proposal review process. Peer review is an important safeguard to ensure that only quality proposals are funded, particularly at federal agencies that are stewards of public tax dollars. Many foundations also use a peer review process. The peer reviewers are usually anonymous, meaning that you don't know who they are. In some cases the review is double-blind, meaning that your identifying information is redacted from your proposal and the reviewers don't know who you are either. The program officer may make funding decisions based on written reviews alone or bring reviewers together in a meeting to further deliberate and rank the proposals as a group. Many agencies perform two levels of review by sending proposals out for ad hoc review and then convening a panel of different scholars that meets in person, or increasingly by videoconference. Some agencies have reviewers/panelists serve for multiyear terms, and others select new reviewers/panelists for every competition.

Funding agencies often ask reviewers to score proposals. For example, the National Institutes of Health requests a score between 1 and 9, with 1 being the highest score. At the National Endowment for the Humanities, the scoring scale is Excellent, Very Good, Good, Some Merit, and Not Considered. In review panel meetings, there is a fairly standard process whereby each panelist is only assigned a portion of the proposals to review (although for smaller pools of proposals every reviewer might read all the proposals). Each panelist is assigned to be a first, second, or possibly third reader for each of their assigned proposals. Panelists also have the option to read any of the proposals under review and comment on them during the review discussion.

Once the reviews and scores are in and the panel is convened, there are different ways that agencies deal with discussing the proposals. In some cases, the lowest-scoring proposals are not reviewed further; in other cases, all proposals are discussed regardless of the scores. The lead reviewer for a given proposal will start the conversation with his analysis of the proposal's strengths and weaknesses, and then the second reviewer takes her turn. Sometimes a third reader is assigned to be the scribe and take notes on the discussion and synthesize them into reviewer comments that go back to the applicant.

After these initial presentations, the floor is open for discussion. The review panel can become an arena for negotiation where an advocate of a certain proposal can persuade the other panelists to see it in a new and more favorable light. Likewise, proposals can drop precipitously in the ranks once the panel starts talking about it. For some agencies, the competition is so stiff that your proposal will not be funded if it does not have a vocal supporter on the panel. We have heard many anecdotes about brutal and contentious review panels where complex Lord of the Flies–style rhetorical and psychological strategies are operationalized among overlapping sets of allies and enemies in an attempt to game the outcomes of the review process. Personally, however, we have never seen these kinds of shenanigans in our review panel experience. Reviewers are typically conscientious, and any debates are respectful and substantive. Program officers go to great lengths to convene reviewers and panels that will do their jobs in good faith, and they are well versed at facilitating and synthesizing panel discussions. The National Institutes of Health has produced an excellent video to illustrate the typical review process at their agency that can be found here: http://public.csr.nih. gov/ApplicantResources/Pages/default.aspx. This is a realistic portrayal that captures the general process and tone of review at other agencies as well.

Most reviewers, as mentioned, are anonymous. Some agencies, such as the National Institutes of Health, publish the names of members of each of their review panels—called Study Sections in NIH parlance—on their website. Foundations frequently list their board or advisory committee members; these may be their proposal reviewers as well. Although in most cases you won't find out exactly who is reviewing your proposal, you can at least find out how specialized the review will be. If this information is not available on the agency website, you can e-mail the program officer to ask, for example: "Will the reviewers be from my specific field of cultural anthropology, from the broader discipline, or from an interdisciplinary sample of the social sciences?" Knowing this will help you decide how much detail you need to include or jettison in your proposal. It will also help you know whether or not to use (or define for nonspecialists) "jargon," or insider language that is particular to your subfield, in your proposal.

Better than trying to find out information about the review process, become a reviewer yourself. Funding agencies are always on the lookout for qualified reviewers. E-mail the relevant program officer and let them know that you would like to serve. Many federal agencies maintain reviewer databases, and sometimes you can apply to be a reviewer by submitting your credentials online. Agencies also find reviewers by inviting former recipients of their awards, looking at who is cited in the proposals under review, or through citation or Google searches. If invitations from federal agencies and foundations are not forthcoming, ask administrators on your campus how you can get involved in reviewing internal faculty seed grant or graduate fellowship competitions.

Do not hesitate to say yes when invited to serve as a proposal reviewer or panelist, and take the job very seriously. Even though the job can be time consuming, reading other people's proposals and seeing how reviewers and panels rate them is an invaluable experience in learning how to write excellent proposals. Getting into the mind-set of a proposal reviewer will give you several "aha" moments about your own proposal writing—for example, that time you forgot to spell check before submitting it one minute and thirty seconds before the deadline; or that time when you weren't totally sure where you could find the historical documents for your project, so you concisely stated "I will visit the archives" in your methods section; or that time that you budgeted for the entire daily federal per diem rate to do eighteen months of ethnographic fieldwork in a remote village in central China.

Apart from getting a glimpse into why some of your previous proposals might have been rejected, you will also have the opportunity to see the contours of the cutting edge of your academic discipline(s). Being a proposal reviewer helps you become more engaged with your disciplinary community as well. Through this work you will become better acquainted with agency program officers, and on a panel you will participate in gratifying intellectual dialogues while meeting and networking with colleagues in your field.

Here are some links to application instructions and online portals to become a reviewer at selected federal agencies:

- National Endowment for the Humanities: https://securegrants.neh.gov/prism/
- National Science Foundation: www.nsf.gov/bfa/dias/policy/merit_review/reviewer.jsp
- National Institutes of Health: http://grants.nih.gov/grants/peer/becoming_peer_reviewer.htm
- National Institutes of Health Early Career Reviewer Program (a program designed explicitly to give junior scholars the opportunity to experience a review panel even if they have no prior NIH funding): http://public.csr.nih.gov/Reviewer-Resources/BecomeAReviewer/Pages/Overview-of-ECR-program.aspx
- Department of Education Office of Postsecondary Education: www2.ed.gov/about/offices/list/ope/trio/seekingfieldreaders.html
- Institute of Museum and Library Services: www.imls.gov/grants/become-reviewer

Dos and Don'ts of Contacting a Program Officer

In the process of investigating a funding agency, there may be questions unanswered after poring over the RFP and website. This is when a well-placed call to a program officer might fill in the gaps of your knowledge and make your proposal more competitive. There are many good reasons to call a program officer, but only after you are sure that the information is not already posted. In fact, many agencies list FAQs precisely to cover all the minor but recurrent questions that they get from prospective applicants.

The motto of many program officers is "Call early and call often." Yet researchers often feel deeply afraid or embarrassed to do so. Some think they might ask a "dumb" question that the program officer will remember when it comes time for proposal review. Some think that if they reveal their research idea and it is not a good fit for the agency, the program officer will shoot them out of the water before they even apply. Yes, it is important to make a good impression on the program officer. But answering "dumb" questions and giving guidance about proposals is standard fare for them. Indeed, it is their job! If you are truly paralyzed by the idea of contacting a program officer, seek advice from your campus Research Development Office. They will assist you in crafting what you say or send to the program officer, and some will even make the phone call for you or with you.

Mind you, program officers are busy, and they are unfortunately not paid to mentor researchers in depth. They cannot in all fairness give significantly more attention or information to any one applicant over another. And some agencies or particular programs are so oversubscribed that the program officer can't possibly manage conversations with every applicant, or even a percentage of them. One example is the National Endowment for the Humanities Fellowship Program.

That being said, we always advise researchers to make appropriate contact with program officers. For starters, if you are not sure if your proposal is a good fit for an agency, e-mail the program officer a "one-pager" well in advance of the proposal deadline (i.e., three to six months before). A "one-pager" is a description of your project that takes up a page or less. Provide information about the theoretical context and significance, the research question(s) and hypothesis(es) or outcomes, and a short description of your methods or plan of work. Although this document is short, it is *not* a document in which to vaguely sketch out your immature ideas and hope they resonate with a program officer. Only send this after you have a well-developed proposal idea and can crystallize it in very short form. We cannot guarantee that a program officer will reply to your "one-pager." But it is worth a try.

For some agencies (foundations in particular), this "one-pager" or Letter of Intent (LOI) is the only way to start the conversation with the agency about your project. If you haven't heard back after two weeks, e-mail them a reminder or give them a phone call. Often you will get very good advice about whether or not your project fits and hopefully tips on ways to improve the focus or direction of the project. They might suggest a more suitable program to apply to at their agency or a different agency altogether. We have worked with program officers who have shared relevant bibliographies and have given us specific guidance on how to interpret RFP language, for instance. Many researchers attest that contacting and/or establishing a professional relationship with a program officer has made the crucial difference between funding and failure.

Formatting a "One-Pager"

The "one-pager" should include the key components of a full proposal, giving the program officer enough information to assess the contribution of the project and your qualifications to accomplish the research. As the name implies, this should fit on one page. However, we have also seen program officers ask for "two-pagers," for example, and many agencies have specific guidelines for LOIs. Regardless of the precise formatting, the following is the information that you want to clearly and briefly impart and a guide for approximately how much space to devote to each section:

- Introduction—basic description of project, including the research question(s) (approximately two to five sentences)
- Theoretical Context and Significance—statement of need (one-third of a page)
- Plan of Work—methodology (one-third of a page)
- Your Qualifications—prior work (approximately two to five sentences)
- Ballpark duration and requested amount (approximately one to two sentences)

Even better than a "one-pager" exchange, make a trip to Washington, DC, or New York or wherever your agency is located and meet the program officer in person. Program officers typically welcome such visits. This is a chance to talk to the program officer about your research ideas, as well as to ask questions about their program, the review process, the current success rates, and the agency more generally. If you can't get to Washington, DC, some program officers routinely attend professional disciplinary conferences and will schedule one-on-one meetings there. Some HSS federal agencies also hold annual conferences throughout the country, such as:

- The National Institutes of Health organizes the NIH Regional Seminar (http://grants.nih.gov/grants/seminars.htm).
- The National Science Foundation organizes NSF Days (www.nsf.gov/events/).
- The National Endowment for the Humanities sends program officers to various universities to conduct regional proposal writing workshops and to consult one-on-one with prospective applicants. These events have been limited in recent years due to funding constraints, but you can contact the NEH to find out their schedule (https://www.neh.gov/about/contact).

Increasingly, agencies have been airing live webinars to disseminate information about their pending programs and to engage in discussions and question–answer sessions with the public. These can be great opportunities to ask questions and become visible to a program officer.

Another appropriate occasion to contact a program officer is after your proposal has been rejected. They can give you an honest assessment of whether it is worth reapplying in the next round or if you should start from scratch with something different. If you haven't received them already, you can ask for reviewer comments (although some foundations, in particular, do not have the staff bandwidth to furnish these). If you receive reviewer comments, the program officer can give you feedback about which critiques to pay more or less attention to. Particularly when the comments are far flung or conflicting, you should ask how to balance these in the rewrite and if the program officer recommends taking one tack over another. Overall, the key is to build a relationship, without being gratuitous, and to glean important "between the lines" information, without pressing for unfair advantage.

Above all, be nice to your program officer. They may have more power than you think in making funding decisions, and you do not want to incur their wrath under any circumstances! Remain professional and courteous; even if you are outraged by unnecessarily scathing reviews; even if they never have the time to call you back; even if your proposal fell half of a percentage point below the funding line. There is no point in burning a bridge with a program officer or funding agency.

Summary

If you are following the logic of this book, you have by now conducted and narrowed your funding search, and you have done your homework to figure out how to write the most competitive proposal possible for your target agency. This chapter explains how to study agency websites and successful proposals to determine if your project will "fit." It also gives you guidance for understanding the typical proposal review process and tips for contacting and communicating with a program officer. You are almost ready to start writing! In the next chapter, we take you through some quick steps that you can take to ensure the most efficient and productive writing experience.

BOX 3.1   FLASH TOPIC: PROGRAM OFFICER VIEWPOINT—NATIONAL ENDOWMENT FOR THE HUMANITIES

By Stefanie Walker, Senior Program Officer, Division of Research Programs, National Endowment for the Humanities*

Eleven Essential Tips for Applying to the National Endowment for the Humanities

1. **Read the guidelines!** NEH guidelines are revised and fine-tuned every year. They include detailed information about how to prepare and submit a proposal. Craft your application to fit the specific set of guidelines of the grant you are aiming for. Do not simply recycle a book prospectus, previous submission, or other grant proposal.
2. Give yourself **enough time** to prepare. Rushed and sloppy applications almost never succeed. Don't wait to submit only hours before the grant deadline. Problems with Grants.gov and other possible snags can cost precious time!
3. Talk to an **NEH program officer**. They are trained to help you and are an excellent resource. Have specific questions ready, based on your reading of the guidelines.

4. Look at the **sample proposals** posted on the NEH website, and ask the program officer for others if there isn't a good fit for your project. Query the online grants database for comparable funded projects.

5. Internalize the **evaluation criteria** posted for each NEH grant opportunity. Make sure the application covers all of them!

6. The **narrative** portion of the proposal must be both specific enough to satisfy a specialist in a given field and clear enough so that a generalist reader can easily grasp the project's significance for the humanities. Be persuasive and up to date, but do not use jargon, and define field-specific concepts and terminology. Balance abstract ideas with one or two well-chosen examples that illustrate your larger point. Anticipate reviewers' concerns and answer them.

7. Research development professionals can help their constituents by **proofreading** NEH grant applications that are submitted by individuals (fellowships, summer stipends, awards for faculty, public scholar). For institutional grants, **send a draft** at least six weeks ahead of the due date to the program officer for feedback.

8. Don't forget a clear and realistic **plan of work** for the requested grant period (and beyond, if the project will not be completed during that time).

9. Make the **budget** realistic, but keep it within the range of previous funding in a given grant program. See the website for recent awards. Cost sharing is not required, but indicating a certain degree of institutional buy-in usually makes a positive impression on reviewers.

10. Projects with a **digital** component or others born digital are ever more popular. Don't claim to (re)invent something unique. Instead, try to use open-access software and ensure that digital material (databases, tools, maps, visualizations, interactive, etc.) will have a long-term presence through a well-conceived sustainability plan.

11. Successful or unsuccessful, request the **peer reviewers' comments**. Revise and resubmit. At NEH, all reviewers change every grant cycle.

* This information is publically available through the National Endowment for the Humanities.

Stefanie Walker has served at National Endowment for the Humanities as a Program Officer since 2008. She is an art historian of European sculpture and decorative arts from the 16th through the 18th centuries.

4

GETTING READY TO WRITE

By now you have identified your sources of funding, you are aware of the institutional rules and procedures for applying for grants and fellowships, and you are finally ready to write the proposal! But before you sit down and get started, we suggest that you organize your schedule, your mind, and your space in a way that will give you the best proposal writing results. There are many great books out there on how to be a productive writer. Here, we briefly touch on some key concepts and provide a list of links and resources for more reading on this topic.

Create a Schedule and a Career Map

When sitting down to write your proposal, you need to think about three different schedules. At the lowest resolution, how does proposal writing and grant funding fit into your longer-term career goals? On another level, what is the proposal writing and submission schedule for each round of funding? At the micro-level, what is your plan for the proposal writing itself?

Use a calendar, use a spreadsheet, use a list, or use a chalkboard on your wall. Find a way that works for you and map out your research destiny in a visual form. First, think about your longer-term plans. For instance, if you are a junior faculty member or graduate student, you should plan out the six-odd years that it will take you to get tenure or the dissertation. Ask yourself these types of questions.

Junior Faculty Member

- What do I need to accomplish to get tenure?
- Can I get my book or articles published based on my dissertation alone?
- When should each article or book be published?
- Will I need research funding to add a new dimension to my project?

- When will I do fieldwork or archival work?
- Can I get the writing done during the summer and in between teaching responsibilities?
- Will I need a year of course release to complete my research or write the book?
- When should I present my work at conferences?
- When should I start preliminary research for my next post-tenure project?

Graduate Student

- What do I need to accomplish to file my dissertation?
- Apart from the dissertation, how many articles do I need to be competitive on the job market?
- When should each article and/or the dissertation be completed?
- What type of funding will I need for each stage of my research, from pre-dissertation to proposal writing?
- When will I do the bulk of my research, whether it is fieldwork, archival work, or close reading?
- Can I get the writing done during the summer and in between coursework and TA responsibilities?
- When should I present my work at conferences?
- When should I start preliminary research for my post-doctoral fellowship or my next early career project?

Think through an optimal long- and medium-term schedule, correlate this with your funding wish list, and start planning. Although this book aims to help you focus on your research goals, we understand that you must do your research within the wider demands of your work and life, whether you are a graduate student, a faculty member, or an unaffiliated scholar who earns a living outside of academia. As such, you might also use this calendar, list, or mental map to put your research into the context of the other responsibilities that you face. How many courses will you teach or take per year, and do you have the option to consolidate these into one term in order to dedicate the other term to writing? How are your family responsibilities distributed over the year? Summer seems like a good chunk of uninterrupted writing time for some people; however, those of us with small children know that the relentless summer camp and swimming lesson chauffeuring schedule can leave only small windows of time each day for productive writing. Of course, you won't stick to this schedule exactly, and things might go awry from time to time. But starting with a plan and checking in with it several times a year to rethink and revise accordingly will help you reach your career and writing goals more quickly.

Within these career road maps, write down the obvious grants and fellowships that you want to apply for, indicating where they fit into your overall long-term schedule and the annual deadlines for each. The majority of agencies and foundations have fairly reliable annual deadlines, but you will also want to do new funding searches a couple of times a year, or subscribe to a funding alerting service, to stay abreast of new and one-off opportunities. Allocate yourself at least three to six months prior to each proposal submission deadline for developing and fine-tuning the proposal. If you plan to branch out into a new research area, you will need even more time to do the necessary background and secondary source research to understand the dimensions and contours of your new topic. Next, for each proposal or set of proposals, identify the following tasks and target dates and put them in your calendar or list:

- Review RFP and direct questions about the opportunity to campus research development staff, sponsored projects staff, or agency program officers.
- Complete first draft to circulate to your colleagues and research development staff for review and feedback
- Time for iterative rewriting and recirculation
- Secure commitments for course buyout, cost-share, letters of reference, etc.
- Subcontract paperwork and coordination with collaborators
- Writing the finishing touches: bibliography, data management plan, and final spell check and editing
- Institutional signatures and forms
- Campus deadline for sponsored projects compliance review
- Agency submission deadline.

Note that collaborative proposals can take exponentially longer to prepare and submit, both for the collaborative proposal writers and the campus administrators who prepare the submission paperwork. We discuss strategies for successful collaborative grantsmanship and research in Chapter 12.

Daily Writing

Once you have a long-term schedule established, it is time to get into your writing groove. There is plenty of good advice out there about how to be a productive writer, and we will not thoroughly review that literature here. Suffice it to say that many experts on the subject agree that you **must establish a daily writing practice**. Although we all admit to a little binge-writing in our pasts (which, quite frankly, can be relatively productive—that's how we have been writing this book, for example), research shows that regular shorter periods of scheduled writing will result in higher overall rates of productivity and more creative ideas.

Robert Boice, a psychologist who specialized in faculty development, led the way on this research, publishing several studies and self-help guidebooks devoted to the practice of productive writing. His work has been taken up by other scholars who have contributed additional self-help books to the genre. If you want to correct your bad binge-writing ways or get through the latest bout of dreaded writer's block, this reading list will get you started:

Boice, R. (1983). Contingency management in writing and the appearance of creative ideas: Implications for the treatment of writing blocks. *Behaviour Research and Therapy, 21*(5), 537–543.

Boice, R. (1990). *Professors as Writers: A Self-Help Guide to Productive Writing.* Stillwater, OK: New Forums Press.

Silvia, P. J. (2007). *How to Write a Lot: A Practical Guide to Productive Academic Writing.* Washington, DC: American Psychological Association.

If you don't have the willpower to go it alone, mutual shaming (er, encouragement!) can help you adhere to a writing schedule. Look for a writing buddy or join a writing accountability group. Your institution may facilitate annual or summer writing groups, or you can find several excellent sources of writing group support online (some charge fees, some are free), a few of which are listed here:

- The National Center for Faculty Development and Diversity (www.facultydiversity. org/) is a professional development, training, and mentoring community of over 18,000 graduate students, post-docs, and faculty members. They offer several programs to motivate writing consistency and success, including writing workshops and retreats, peer mentoring, accountability buddy matches, monthly writing challenges, and more.
- Academic Writing Club (http://academicwritingclub.com/) offers a structured, online, coaching system that includes a combination of accountability tools and productivity coaching designed to jumpstart your writing. You work with a supportive online community of experts and colleagues to develop and maintain ideal writing habits.
- Summer Academic Working Groups (http://jayandleanne.com/lpowner/ pages/sawg/), organized by Leanne Powner, is a forum that allows academics to collaborate electronically for feedback and mutual accountability during the summer. Participants are divided into clusters of four to six individuals in the same academic division who share work in progress on a regular basis and provide each other with feedback.

Some of our colleagues swear by writing timers, and the Web is awash in cute and entertaining ways to incentivize you to sit down and write for twenty minutes or 200 words at a time. Try:

- The Pomodoro Technique (www.pomodorotechnique.com/) if you like tomatoes
- Tick Tock Timer (http://ticktocktimer.com/) if you like the sounds of gongs
- Written? Kitten! (http://writtenkitten.net/) if you love adorable baby cats
- Write or Die (http://writeordie.com/) if you respond better to punishment than rewards

A Space for Writing

Along with establishing and maintaining a regular writing schedule, we want to mention one other strategy that can help you achieve your writing goals: create the right physical space for writing. Figure out where and when you write best and what will help you stay in front of the computer. Put these writing appointments in your calendar, and treat them as you would any other important meetings that you attend on the job. Surround yourself with the necessary resources so that you won't be lured away by frequent needs and desires. Assemble your materials. Have the grant RFP and some sample successful proposals handy for reference. Working on the theoretical significance section today? Make sure that you have copies of the relevant literature readily accessible—either online or in a stack of printed books and journal articles on your desk. If you are writing a proposal to do field research in Ouagadougou, for example, set the mood by hanging a map of West Africa in your office. And don't forget the jug of water, the cup of coffee, and the container of snacks. Once you have your optimal setting in place, minimize distractions. Turn off your phone. Exit your e-mail software. Close the door.

Now set that timer and start writing your proposal!

All that Internet research and preparatory homework has paid off. Now is the time to take your research idea and turn it into a coherent and fundable proposal. In the next chapter we walk you through one of the most difficult proposal writing blocks: narrowing your research interests down to a compelling scholarly research question.

Summary

Writing can be hard. Fitting it into a busy academic work schedule makes it even more challenging. However, there are some simple strategies you can employ to help you succeed. First, write up or draw out a plan and refer to it frequently to stay on track. Then, use well-known techniques for productive writing. Write *daily*, and give yourself the space and other resources that will make you stay put and write. In the next chapter we help you begin to crystallize your research ideas into a coherent and compelling funding proposal.

Bibliography

Boice, R. (1983). Contingency management in writing and the appearance of creative ideas: Implications for the treatment of writing blocks. *Behaviour Research and Therapy, 21*(5), 537–543.

Boice, R. (1990). *Professors as Writers: A Self-Help Guide to Productive Writing.* Stillwater, OK: New Forums Press.

Silvia, P. J. (2007). *How to Write a Lot: A Practical Guide to Productive Academic Writing.* Washington, DC: American Psychological Association.

5

FOCUSING THE RESEARCH IDEA AS GRANT OR FELLOWSHIP PROPOSAL

Whether you have a well-developed research plan or are just beginning a new research endeavor, it is important to understand that proposal writing is a genre that differs in significant ways from a journal manuscript, a book chapter, and other forms of academic writing. Proposals are persuasive and formulaic documents that must adhere to specific expectations and norms in the research funding world. It is often frustrating for scholars to take their vast knowledge and creative thinking and distill it into a concise, tightly argued, and detailed research proposal.

This chapter will take you through the process of zeroing in on the most sellable research idea that stays true to your academic goals. Don't forget that "selling" your idea is key here, as distasteful as that may sound to the ears of an earnest intellectual. Recall the bleak headlines that we mentioned in previous chapters: dwindling sources of funding, success rates hovering in the teens, conscientious review panels . . . in this environment, you can't just blithely describe your brilliant research idea and expect it to speak for itself. No, you need to devise an overall strategy to determine what the agencies want to fund and how to write a proposal that speaks to the intended audience. We will discuss the second half of this strategy—the writing—in Chapters 6 through 11. Here we focus on how to tailor your overall research idea to be compelling to funding agencies.

The process of how to hit the sweet spot of a good research project cannot be boiled down to a step-by-step manifesto for action. It will always depend on the idiosyncrasies of your particular research discipline and your target funding agency. On top of that, the project will be fundamentally defined by how much money is available to carry out the work.

Nevertheless, we can generalize enough to say that a good research idea is a combination of:

- Your scholarly interests
- A thorough understanding of the existing and cutting-edge literature or work in your field and how your project fits into it

- A good measure of scholarly creativity, which is what distinguishes your project as a major contribution
- A feasible plan of work
- A reasonable budget

For the majority of academic funders, the contribution of your research should be "theoretical"—meaning that your research outcome should change what we know and how we think about (your topic inserted here).

What precisely do we mean by a "theoretically significant contribution?" Some disciplines do not explicitly engage the term "theory." Throughout this book, however, we use the terms "theory" and "theoretical" to capture the range of common and accepted knowledge, paradigms, and conventions of thought in any given discipline or field of study. You might translate "theory" to:

- The scholarly context for your research
- The existing literature on your topic to which you are contributing

Often a theoretical contribution is shaped by novel empirical evidence or the application of new methods, for example, but the crux of the proposal must revolve around theoretical significance and rigor. (With that said, several agencies only fund more practical or applied research projects, which should nevertheless be theoretically well informed, and we discuss those in Chapter 13.) Many agencies publish their evaluation criteria on their RFPs or on their websites, and these reflect the most important merits upon which your project will be judged. For example, the National Science Foundation asks their reviewers to assess first and foremost:

> What is the potential for the proposed activity to . . . advance knowledge and understanding within its own field or across different fields (Intellectual Merit); and . . . To what extent do the proposed activities suggest and explore creative, original, or potentially transformative concepts?

The National Endowment for the Humanities asks reviewers to evaluate primarily "[t]he intellectual significance of the proposed project, including its value to humanities scholars, general audiences, or both."

Thus, a good research project will:

- Substantively fill a gap in the theoretical literature
- Clarify or resolve debates
- Build on and advance knowledge in your field
- Bring theories, methods, approaches, or materials together in novel and significant ways
- Incrementally or extensively shift a paradigm

As such, the first step in developing your research idea is to read everything that has been written on your research topic, from the seminal books and journal articles, up to the cutting-edge work being produced today. Assess the strengths and weaknesses in your field. Look for areas where others have posed critiques and future directions for inquiry. Think through the ways that your research reveals new patterns that are not accommodated by current understandings in your topic area.

Through this review, you will begin to formulate how you can add a new dimension to your theoretical field, for example, by:

- Conducting research in a new field site
- Reanalyzing established paradigms under recent social and economic trends
- Analyzing previously ignored archives, materials, or subjects
- Combining methodologies or procedures in new ways

Through this process you will discover how your project will fill a niche and make a significant contribution to the existing literature.

This is not to say that you have to (or ever will for that matter) think up a new and far-reaching paradigm, theory, or body of work that completely renews our understanding of "economics" or "culture" or "justice," for example. Although there may be a handful of discipline-altering Keyneses, Hurstons, and Foucaults among us, it is more probable that your work will contribute to a specific research area as it moves through larger collective scholarly transformations. Especially as a graduate student or junior faculty member, it is best not to claim that you are inventing a new theory or paradigm in your research proposals. Coining new terms can also be seen as overly precocious. Oftentimes this kind of hyperbole merely masks the fact that you haven't read all the pertinent literature.

Narrowing your diverse scholarly interests down to a research proposal involves considerable editing of your thoughts. Common critiques of graduate student and junior faculty proposals include "This project is too ambitious," or "The researcher can't complete the scope of work in the funding period." These statements are symptomatic of novice researchers not knowing how to gauge the scale of what actually goes into a research project and thinking they need to lay out everything they've got in order to impress the reviewers.

What Your Research Idea Should Not Be

In describing what a research idea should be, it is instructive to explain what a research idea shouldn't be. Do not propose to merely fill a gap that is empirical or descriptive. In other words, just because a research project hasn't been done before doesn't mean it is a good research project.

For example, your project should not replicate another person's research in a different village simply because no one has studied that village before. Not unless there is something about the history of the village, or the people who live there, etc., that changes what we know from prior studies about your theoretical field. Similarly, you should not set out to write the history of bubble gum just because the Bazooka archives have never been plumbed by a historian. Although this could be fun and interesting, such a descriptive study would not be attractive to funders (besides the Bazooka Foundation) unless you can make the theoretical argument that, for example, bubble gum sales and marketing discourses have played an essential role in shaping American youth culture, which provides a counternarrative to how scholars have previously theorized American youth culture. We know you are creative, but don't propose to do a project that has sprung from your consciousness in a vacuum as though it is the very first of its kind. Every research project has a context and antecedents against which you juxtapose your current project. How will your project expand, build on, question, etc., the genre in which you are working in meaningful ways?

This brings up another problem we often see in research proposals: a scholar proposes to go off to the field, the archive, the lab, etc., "to see what they can see." As social scientists and humanists, we sometimes don't want to influence our research findings with an overly prescriptive research plan, or set of questions, or list of hypotheses. However, you will not be competitive in winning grants and fellowships these days if you have no clue about what you are going to find in your research. There are too many scholars applying for the same grant who have already managed to do preliminary research, who know enough about their field site, their dataset, the contents of the Bazooka archive, for example, that they can present a convincing narrative about the anticipated significance of their project. No agency can afford to give you funding without some assurance of bang for the buck. And as a graduate student or junior faculty member, you do not have yet the track record to win a grant by way of a "trust me" proposal.

A third mistake that is common to research projects is when a scholar writes a persuasive essay as opposed to asking a question and then explaining how she will answer it. This kind of proposal has its place if you are requesting funding to do the final stages of writing your book or dissertation. Your data are collected, your research questions are answered, and you already know what the book is going to be about. In this case, summarizing the arc of your argument in a proposal would be appropriate. Even in these kinds of proposals, however, you should discuss your original research questions and how you went about answering them. However, if you are requesting funding to do *research*, then you cannot provide the agency with a proposal that reads more like a journal article, with a $100,000 budget tacked on at the end. Some scholars do this because they simply believe that they should get a big grant on the basis of their sheer intellect or past contributions to their field. It is more apt for these scholars to apply for, or be nominated for, prizes, awards, or endowed chairs, as opposed to research grants and fellowships.

But this phenomenon also hints at a somewhat common, but potentially unethical, practice in research and proposal writing: that of submitting a proposal to conduct research that you have already done. We have heard many scholars swear by the "30% rule." This means when writing a proposal, 30% of the proposed work should be completed, 30% should be in progress, and 30% would be done with the new grant. As scholars, we are continuously engaged in research and creative work throughout our careers. Thus to some extent this formula makes sense. Research is never really finished; it just morphs into the next project. So by all means, collect a little extra data during your current funding that will lead to formulating the next research proposal. This is not a crime. But requesting funding for work that is already completed (even if not published), particularly if it was already substantively funded by a prior grant or fellowship, is crossing the line and should not be attempted.

Fourth, another area to edit judiciously is the amount of complexity involved in your research. Complexity is not easy to convey in a proposal. The conditions under which reviewers read proposals do not engender the most thorough tracking of your every word. Reviewers (as we allude to throughout this book) have little time, they are not getting paid, and they are looking for reasons to ding you. As a result they have no patience for a proposal that requires them to do heavy analysis and mind-bending memorization to keep track of your multipronged project. Infographics can help communicate complexity, but to the extent possible, you should avoid putting too much into your proposal. Do you really need to explain every twist and turn of the political history in Beijing to set up your research on contemporary post-Marxist worker's unions? Although small details may play out in your eventual analysis, leave the minutiae for your monograph. Similarly, the results of your research may have implications for several sets of theoretical areas, some more obscure than others. Leave the obscure ones out. When you get funded, feel free to explore every possible data point and hypothesis and far-reaching theoretical contribution that you can imagine. But in the proposal, focus on the bolder strokes, particularly those that will resonate with the target reviewers and agencies.

Finally, as a graduate student or junior faculty member, do not submit an academic proposal, which if funded, will save the world, provide shelter for orphans, or bring about global peace. In other words, your work as a scholar is not development work, nor is it nonprofit programming. Every agency loves to see some societal relevance in a proposal (what the National Science Foundation calls "broader impacts"), but this cannot be the main goal or result of your research, unless you are applying for a grant that would fund this kind of work. But then this would not be categorized as academic research, and it would be more prudent perhaps to establish a nonprofit organization as a side business. Many problems in our world could benefit from research and analysis, and you may well be inclined to ameliorate these problems by applying your scholarly expertise to them. This kind of research can have a place in your academic career at certain stages (hint: post-tenure) and with certain funding agencies. We talk more about this in Chapter 13. In the early stages of your career, focus more on the scholarly, theoretical, and intellectual contributions that you can make to your academic discipline.

Following Your Passion or Following the Money?

Have you tried multiple times to get your research funded without success? Although you may be writing an excellent research proposal, it is possible that your research is simply not of current interest to funding agencies. An important part of conceptualizing your research project is answering the simple question: "Who cares?" As passionate as you may be about your topic, if you are the only one who sees its value, then it will never get funded. Thus, to a certain extent, scholars need to adjust their research projects to match what is currently being funded. This does not necessarily mean that you have to "sell out" or take up the new and trendy method in your field. But you do need to be realistic enough to stretch the dimensions and contours of your research interests to get them into the realm of possible funding. And you never know: that new method might be an interesting way to reformulate your research, so be open to the possibilities as you assess your opportunities for funding.

In many of the HSS disciplines, some of the biggest theoretical shifts have been precipitated by changes in society and technology. In turn, funding agencies respond to these pragmatic societal shifts in their funding priorities, and the infusion of research funding then reshapes the trajectory of cutting-edge scholarly research. Take, for instance, the recent surge in funding for studies of the societal and cultural implications of new technologies. Likewise, there seems to be no end to the current funding available to understand relationships between society and the environment. The humanities has seen a boost in funding for digital humanities as humanists find a foothold in using computational tools to understand historic and written materials. We also see more opportunities for interdisciplinary, multi-investigator "team science"—which brings scholars together from across the HSS and STEM disciplines—to solve particularly complex and intractable problems.

Pay attention to these trends by studying funding agency reports and RFP language. Many federal agencies and private foundations post annual reports and planning documents. In 2011, for example, the National Science Foundation conducted a visioning process to chart the course of social science research into the next decade. The report, *Rebuilding the Mosaic*, is available online. Each NSF program also creates a periodic strategic plan, and many of these are posted online as well. If you can't locate the one for your target program, request a copy from your program officer. Each center and institute at the National Institutes of Health publishes strategic plans and vision reports, available online (http://report.nih.gov/strategicplans/). The National Endowment for the Humanities also publishes their current strategic plan (www.neh.gov/about/legal/strategic-plan). Similarly, foundations typically post their annual reports, which often synthesize their current priorities and allude to future directions.

Along with gleaning information about current and future funding trends in these reports, you should pay attention to what has been funded by agencies in the last few years. Consider where your project fits in (or does it not fit at all?). Think about ways to integrate emerging funding themes with your research interests. Can you rethink the theoretical significance of your project to shed light on a different area of theory that seems to have more traction in currently funded projects? Are there comparative projects that you can initiate to bridge your old research with an exciting new direction? Are there ways that you can collaborate with colleagues to apply new data, methods, and analyses to your research?

In sum, you will need to do some amount of tailoring your project to meet the expectations and desires of the funding agency. Your proposal is a conversation with them, and your research ideas should be formulated in an iterative process that eventually finds a middle ground between what you really want to do and what will actually be funded.

Applying to Multiple Funders

Some of us are in the lucky position of having a research project that could be funded by several different agencies. This is particularly true when our research is interdisciplinary. However, do not make the mistake of sending every agency the exact same proposal. You will need to go through the process of studying every funder and revise your proposal appropriately for each. Each proposal might involve a different page length, different formatting, responses to different types of prompts and questions, a different central theme or focus of the RFP. Anticipate that this will take a good amount of time, so plan accordingly. It can be especially challenging to revise a fifteen-page proposal down to a three-page proposal, and vice versa. Do not leave this until the week before the deadline.

Unlike submitting journal articles, there are no restrictions against submitting essentially the same proposal to multiple agencies. Many agencies request a listing of current and pending support as part of the application, and they will follow up with you on the status of your pending proposals should they decide to award you a grant. If you are fortunate enough to receive more than one grant or fellowship for the same project, however, the agencies may ask you to choose one over the other or take partial amounts from each. The latter solution is usually preferred so that you can list more grants and fellowships on your curriculum vitae. However, there may be other administrative or regulatory reasons why choosing one over the other makes more sense. Talk through the options with your colleagues, advisors, campus Research Development Office, or Sponsored Projects Office to understand the broader implications of your choices.

Selling Interdisciplinary Research

Although it is a blessing to be eligible for multiple funding opportunities because of your interdisciplinary research project, be aware that many review panels are discipline based and thus not always equipped to evaluate interdisciplinary work. As mentioned in Chapter 3, assess the mission of the agency and composition of the review panel and write your proposal accordingly. For example, if your research is considered "humanistic social sciences," do not emphasize the social science methods if you are applying to the National Endowment for the Humanities. If your research could just as easily be funded by the National Geographic Society and the Wenner-Gren Foundation, by all means highlight your contributions to geography in the National Geographic Society proposal and your anthropological contributions in the Wenner-Gren proposal. Your ability to speak across the disciplines may be impressive, but this is not always easy to translate to a review panel that only speaks the language of one of your disciplines. As we discuss earlier, edit, remove unnecessary complexity, and focus on giving the agency and reviewers what they want.

Summary

Honing in on the most sellable research project requires editing your ideas for clarity and simplicity. The majority of academic funding agencies are seeking projects that make a scholarly contribution to your field of research and are not just descriptive or empirical. Think carefully about how your project will address the mission of your target agency and the interests of the reviewers. Be aware that your research interests may not be desirable because of current trends or target areas in your discipline or at the funding agencies. You may need to adjust your project slightly to match what is currently fundable.

Now that you have a better sense of the significance of your research project, formulated in direct relation to the mission of your target funding agency(ies), it is time to begin systematically writing the key sections of your proposal. In the next chapters of this book, we teach you formatting and rhetorical strategies for the most common and important proposal sections.

BOX 5.1   FLASH TOPIC: PROGRAM OFFICER VIEWPOINT—FOUNDATIONS

By Joseph S. Meisel, Deputy Provost, Brown University

Reading Proposals

During the eleven years I spent as a foundation program officer, I read thousands of proposals and worked closely with prospective grantees on further developing their proposals before recommending them to our board. For me, reading proposals was not simply a matter of evaluating fit with the funding program's criteria and objectives, or even whether the project met the program's highest aspirations. Proposals also needed to help me answer the fundamental question: "Why fund this and not that?"

To make their case, then, proposals must convey not only an understanding of the foundation's programmatic objectives and the importance of the ideas being advanced in relation to those objectives, but also the investigators' capabilities for carrying out the activities proposed and an organizational scheme that shows how things will work. A strong combination of all these elements both helped to persuade me that a project was a good candidate for funding and helped me to explain "why this" to the foundation's senior leadership and ultimately the board.

In my experience, the most effective proposals typically included the following elements:

- *A clearly defined central problem or set of questions.* These could be of a practical, institutional nature, or they could be issues in scholarship being pursued by an individual investigator or group of investigators. A coherent and focused definition of what the work proposed is responding to and means to accomplish is crucial for understanding both the significance of the project and why funding is needed to pursue it.
- *Well-grounded claims for how the project could make a difference.* This could involve the outcomes of antecedent pilot experiments, hypotheses based on relevant models, analysis of high-quality data, and even arguments from common sense. This is not to say that I looked only for projects where the stated outcomes were virtually guaranteed. At the other extreme, proposals based on airy speculation or uncritical acceptance of dogmas were not persuasive. Foundation funding is a type of risk capital, so it was important to make recommendations with some basis for thinking that the effort was worthwhile and good outcomes were likely—even if the project ultimately fell short of its principal objectives.
- *Project leadership with appropriate expertise and experience.* It's important to see not only that the applicant is capable of carrying out the work proposed, but also that she or he has what it takes to deliver on the project's claims to significance. In the case of an institutional grant, the principal investigator (PI) must be someone in a position of appropriate authority. In the case of an individual or collaborative project grant, program officers need to judge the investigators' background and track record. They also need to see that the institutions involved possess the right infrastructure for supporting the work. Foundations look for excellent ideas, but it is equally vital to assess capability for bringing them to fruition. From the perspective of reading proposals, project leadership also involves not leaving the articulation of a proposal's central rationale and substance to others such as the professional development staff or those writing letters of support or recommendation.
- *A solid plan of organization and justification for funding.* It's actually not enough to have great ideas and to be eminently qualified to do the work. The proposal has to demonstrate the investigator's skills as an intellectual organizer by conceiving the right structure of activities that will allow the stated objectives to be achieved. Related to this, it's no good asking for funding if it's not clear why and for what the funds are needed. The project plan and budget should be of a piece with the "ideas" part of the proposal, not just tacked on randomly at the close. Ultimately, the proposal reader needs to be able to envision how the project would actually work in practice and how the funding requested would help make it happen.

As a genre, grant proposals privilege clarity of ideas and plans. The demand for such clarity—as exemplified by the qualities I've described here—ideally turns the exercise of writing proposals into a significant stage in strengthening a project's conceptualization.

Joseph S. Meisel worked at The Andrew W. Mellon Foundation as Program Officer for Research Universities and Humanistic Scholarship from 1999 to 2010. He is a historian of modern Britain.

PART II

Parts of the Proposal

6

WRITING A STRATEGIC PROPOSAL

No matter how brilliant your research project might be, if it is disguised in a poorly written proposal, it will never be funded. As we have insisted throughout this book, proposal writing is not creative writing; nor is it the same as writing a journal article or book chapter. A proposal is written for a specific audience and must follow the guidelines of a specific request for proposals (RFP). Writing a proposal is formulaic at its core. Once you learn the formula, you will be able to adapt it to different projects, different agencies, and different proposal formats with ease. This chapter will help you decide how to format your project description to best meet the agency RFP and write in a way that makes reviewers happy.

The more proposals you write and read, the more you will see that they follow a common pattern. This does not mean that there is a one-size-fits-all solution to every proposal. And it does not mean that every successful proposal follows the same formula. However, as a novice to proposal writing, we suggest that you begin your process by following our recipe. Using the heuristic that we describe will at least enable you to develop a systematic and thorough proposal. Once you have cracked the basic code, feel free to embellish, rearrange, or reject some of our ideas.

Over the next five chapters, we explain best practices, rhetorical strategies, and writing formulas for each section of a typical proposal. We also provide several examples of successful proposal sections from various HSS disciplines. One of your paramount goals is to make your proposal easy to read. The proposal should be formatted to make your terrific ideas stand out and to help reviewers easily see your proposal in the most favorable light.

You do not want the program officer or reviewer to have to think very hard to figure out your proposal. They should not become frustrated halfway through because you have not yet told them what you are going to do in your research project. They should not have to look up words on Wikipedia to understand your research questions or theoretical contributions. They should not have to explain your proposal to a review panel better than you have explained it your-self. For the most part, no one is going to give you the benefit of the doubt or let small errors slide. Reviewers want easy answers to critical questions about your proposal, such as:

- What is the problem?
- What is the question?
- What is the point?
- Who cares?
- So what?
- Who is this guy/gal?

Let's start with the three most common reasons for a rejected proposal:

- You wrote your proposal at the last minute
- Your project is not a good fit for your target funding agency
- You didn't follow the directions in the RFP

Is the deadline several weeks away? Do you understand what your target agency wants? Have you studied the review process? Have you read the small print where they tell you precisely which font and margin size to use? If not, please go back and read Chapters 3 and 4 first. There is no point in sitting down to write your proposal if you haven't done your homework about the agency or allowed yourself enough time to develop a quality proposal.

The Sequence of a Proposal: Conceptualizing vs. Writing

Proposals follow a typical pattern. Most RFPs will ask for the same types of information, organized in a fairly standard way. The most common sections and sequence are as follows:

1. Summary/Abstract
2. Project Description/Narrative
    a. Introduction/Statement of Problem/Statement of Purpose
    b. Theoretical Orientation/Conceptual Framework and Significance
    c. Methodology/Plan of Work/Data Analysis
    d. Timeline
    e. Dissemination of Results
    f. Qualifications of Researcher/Team
3. Budget
4. Budget Justification
5. References or Bibliography
6. Appendices (such as Evaluation Plan, Data Management Plan, Data Collection Instruments, etc.)

These are not the only sections that you will see in grant and fellowship proposals, and many agencies will not require all of these elements. But this list will help you understand the essential elements of a proposal and how they fit together.

Although this is a common format for a finished and polished proposal, it is not necessarily the way that you should conceptualize and write your proposal, and in fact it does not follow the sequence in which you think through the elements of your research project. Instead, proposal development more often goes something like this:

1.   Theoretical Orientation/Conceptual Framework and Significance

What precisely do we mean by Theoretical Orientation and Conceptual Framework? It boils down to this:

- What is the scholarly context for your research?
- What is the existing literature on your topic to which you are contributing?
- How does your research build on or change what is known about your topic?

Some disciplines do not explicitly engage the term "theory." Throughout this book, however, we use the term "theory" and "theoretical" to capture the range of common and accepted knowledge, paradigms, and conventions of thought in any given discipline or field of study.

The bottom line is that if you have not identified the contribution that your research makes to existing knowledge in your area, then stop right here and go back to read more of the literature. A key section of your proposal is the theoretical significance. This is the main factor by which your proposal is judged. Therefore, it should be the central theme around which you build your proposal, and every other proposal component will follow from it. You cannot begin writing a proposal if you have not first done enough homework to comprehend the breadth and depth of your chosen field and how your research will make a substantive contribution to it.

2.   Budget

The next important consideration in developing your proposal is the budget. How much funding is available for your project? The amount of funding available will fundamentally determine how much and what types of work you can actually do, and thus your methods and work plan.

Imagine you are interested in studying the effects of climate change on women. What does $300,000, $50,000, and $5,000 get you?

- With a $300,000 grant, you could reasonably conduct fieldwork in multiple field sites over two years with time and funds for several complementary data collection methods or experiments, hire a graduate student or post-doc, and perhaps pay for summer salary and conference attendance.

- With $50,000 your project is much more limited in space and time. You might conduct a national online or telephone survey and hire a part-time student assistant.
- But $5,000 is only enough to conduct a pilot study among a small locally accessible sample of informants, or perhaps a short trip to your intended field site to collect preliminary data.

Thus, in a very practical sense, you will need to adjust the scope of your project to match the allotted budget. The timeline will also be determined by both the budget and sometimes by the agency. Many fellowships, for example, are for one year only. Others provide funding for multiple years. You will need to understand the limits of a reasonable budget at your target agency before you can begin to devise your methodology or plan of work.

3. Methodology/Plan of Work

Now that you know your contribution and the amount of money that you will likely have at your disposal, you can begin to think through the actual plan of work. What are the data, materials, or pieces of evidence required to answer your research questions? What are the standards in your discipline for collecting and analyzing data or studying various types of materials? What can you accomplish given the budgetary constraints on your project?

Once these three substantive sections of the proposal have been conceptualized and drafted—theoretical contribution, budget, and methodology—the remaining sections of the proposal will follow:

4. Timeline
5. Budget Justification
6. Dissemination of Results
7. Qualifications of PI/Team
8. References or Bibliography
9. Appendices

It is often the case that you will work iteratively on all the sections, for example, adjusting the timeline as your methods section comes together, or revising the theoretical context and justification section after you write the methods section, as you realize how much you can accomplish with your proposed dataset or materials.

10. Introduction/Statement of Problem/Statement of Purpose
11. Summary/Abstract

The introduction and summary/abstract sections won't come together until the end, as they need to capture the key parts of the entire proposal. Although you may be working iteratively on the introduction of your proposal throughout the overall writing process, it is not until the proposal is almost complete that you will be able to craft this in the most compelling and concise way. For those writers among us who are linear thinkers and can't possibly move on to the next section until the prior section is complete, it may be useful to draft out the introduction at the very beginning. But don't get stuck on the introduction and let it stand in the way of moving on to the other parts as we describe earlier (if you are having trouble with this, you might try reading the advice of Peter Elbow—see the Flash Topic on "freewriting."). If you do start your proposal writing process with the introduction, just know that it will act as placeholder language and will probably be transformed considerably by the time you finish your final draft. The summary or abstract is typically an abridged version of the introduction, laying out the key points of the proposal. Some agencies have specific guidelines for what to include in this section. The National Science Foundation, for example, requires both "Intellectual Merit" and "Broader Impacts" subsections within the proposal summary.

Also be aware that the abstract or summary is sometimes used in specific ways by the funding agency. If a program officer is not familiar with your area of research, they might use the summary as the basis for seeking potential reviewers for your proposal. If this is the case, you want to make sure that the abstract/summary includes the most appropriate search terms that characterize your research. Be clear in the summary/abstract about your specific area of research within your discipline. Additionally, if funded, the abstract or summary will become the face of your project on the agency's website and in other documents such as their annual report. In this respect, write the summary/abstract strategically to communicate your research to the public. This has become increasingly important in recent years as federal research funding is more scrutinized by politicians and taxpayers, who may only have access to your research summary or abstract.

Weaving the Parts Together Into a Coherent Whole

The process of writing a proposal is iterative, and developments in some sections of a proposal will precipitate a rewrite of other sections. Through all the iterations, it is crucial to maintain consistency across all the proposal sections. For example, when you state in your methods section that you will interview 300 farmers in Chile over six months, make sure that your budget includes living expenses in Chile for six months and human subjects payments for 300 people. If you summarize in your introduction that your methods will include focus groups, cortisol tests, and video observation, do not forget to explain each of these methods in your methods section. This advice sounds obvious, but this is a common mistake in proposals.

Beyond synching the nuts and bolts of the proposal, there must also be a tight correlation between your research questions, your theoretical contribution, and your methods or plan of work. A tried and true technique for lining up these crucial proposal parts is to illustrate them. At this stage in your writing, for both your

TABLE 6.1 Visualizing Your Research Project in a Table

Theoretical Contribution	Research Question(s)	Data/Evidence/ Materials	Data Collection Method/Procedure	Analysis
Contribution 1				
Contribution 2				

sanity and edification, it is helpful to take out a big piece of blank paper, tape it to the wall of your writing space, and begin to draw out or map the various components of your research. This diagram, map, or picture can take different forms. One way to illustrate it is in a matrix as in Table 6.1.

Another way to think it through is with a "mental" or "mind" map, such as:

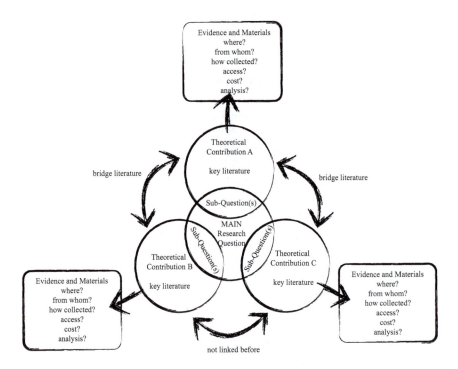

FIGURE 6.1 Visualizing Your Research Project in a Mental Map

Start with these templates to figure out what your research plan looks like in your own head. Show your close colleagues or members of your writing group and see if it makes sense to them. As with the proposal itself, your mental map or matrix will no doubt change over time, and it will not be so tidy that every idea or component fits perfectly into the picture. But every new version will help you refine your concepts and research plan. Having this posted on the wall nearby will keep you on track when you can't see the forest for the trees in your writing process. Eventually, your illustration (professionally rendered) might become a useful infographic device pasted into the proposal itself, particularly if you are working on a longer proposal of roughly ten or more pages.

Use Headers and Mirror the RFP Language

Even in a short, two-page proposal, use headers. The reviewers will thank you. Headers break up the monotony of a page, and they help reviewers see the road map of your project without effort. If your proposal is particularly long (the National Science Foundation, for example, allows fifteen pages, the William T. Grant Foundation twenty), it may be useful to also use subheaders and even a multilevel numbering system to help the reviewer reference where they are throughout a complex proposal.

Every RFP is written differently, and many agencies want specific headers and sections. Other agencies only hint at the vaguest of guidelines and expect you to figure it out yourself. Writing a proposal without any guideposts along the way takes the reviewer on a wild goose chase, wondering what they will encounter around the next bend, paragraph, or page, while trying desperately to put the pieces together in their minds and make sense of the whole.

Reviewers are typically required to write a review of the proposal, summarizing the project and commenting on its strengths and weaknesses. They can't just take a pass on the bad proposals and tell the program officer, "I couldn't even figure that one out." So you can be sure that the more mental calisthenics that they have to do in reading your proposal, the more irritated they will be, and the lower your score will sink in the ratings.

Do all winning proposals use headers? No. But we are big fans of them anyway. Especially for the novice proposal writer, dividing your project into sections can help you think through the nuances of your research design and the ways in which your research questions, theoretical contributions, and methods triangulate in a way that makes the most sense.

Ettenberg's Trick

Related to headers and overall formatting strategies, we cannot overstate the benefits of white space in your proposal. Give the reviewers a break by avoiding wall-to-wall text on every page. Some of you might argue that you need every last square inch to fit in all the information necessary to convey your project. However, consider this: if your proposal is ten pages of dense, unrelenting text, the reviewer may well not read the entire thing anyway. To open up the proposal and give it and the reviewer some breathing room, try Ettenberg's Trick. This formatting device was taught to us by UC Santa Barbara Professor of Psychological and Brain Sciences Aaron Ettenberg. He recommends the following:

1. Write your proposal in 14-point font
2. Make the narrative fit within the prescribed page limits, editing judiciously to maintain the 14-point font.
3. Once everything fits, change the font to 12 point (or whatever is allowable in your RFP guidelines). This should give you a couple of extra pages to work with.
4. Don't fill in this newly discovered white space with more text! Use it instead for illustrations, diagrams, photos, tables, and extra lines between paragraphs or sections. We promise—your reviewer will thank you!

Decoding RFPs

Let's look at some samples from a selection of the standard HSS RFPs and interpret the RFP language. For each of the following funding opportunities, we highlight the precise language that instructs you in how to write the project description.[1] Notice the variation in language, but also notice that they are all essentially asking for the same information:

*   A research question or statement
*   The theoretical significance
*   Methods
*   Timeline
*   Outcomes
*   Qualifications of the investigator

The National Endowment for the Humanities Fellowship

Narrative—Not to Exceed Three Single-Spaced Pages

The narrative should provide an intellectual justification for your project, addressing the four areas listed below: research and contribution; methods and work plan; competencies, skills, and access; and final product and dissemination. A simple statement of need or intent is insufficient. The narrative should not assume specialized knowledge and should be free of technical terms and jargon.

The description goes on to give specific guidance for each of the four sections. Compared to many HSS agencies, the National Endowment for the Humanities provides very thorough instructions for writing your proposal and strongly suggests formatting and headers for the information required. These are closely aligned with the typical proposal sections and sequence that we describe earlier. By all means, structure your writing with the headers that they suggest:

Section 1 header: **Research and Contribution**
Section 2 header: **Methods and Work Plan**

Section 3 header: **Competencies, Skills, and Access**
Section 4 header: **Final Product and Dissemination**

This is the information that the reviewers will be looking for. Why make it difficult for them to find? Even in a three-page proposal, changes in content and flow between paragraphs can be difficult to discern for someone who has already read thirteen proposals before yours and is fighting the strong inclination to fall asleep, despite the sound of a howling baby two rows back, on a flight from LAX to Reagan National. (Yes, this is a typical scene in the life of a proposal reviewer; planes are a common location for getting this kind of academic work done).

The American Council of Learned Societies Fellowships

Content (The proposal must not exceed five double-spaced pages):

A concise statement describing your research project is required. The narrative statement should explain, briefly but specifically, what you plan to do and why, as well as describe progress already made, make clear the relevance of the project to your professional experience, and discuss the significance of this work within your specific and general fields. Please balance the description of specific work plans against an overview of your goals and the contribution this project will make to the field(s) it engages. Please title your proposal in a brief, descriptive way and label sections of your narrative as appropriate to assist readers.

The American Council of Learned Societies provides somewhat less prescription and structure than other agencies, but this does not mean that you should write a rambling five-page stream of consciousness essay that somehow touches on all of these elements, with no breaks or guidelines for the reviewers. In fact, the American Council for Learned Societies asks you to "Please . . . label sections of your narrative as appropriate to assist readers." When encountering an RFP such as this, begin by breaking down their instructions into potential sections and headers. By transforming the earlier paragraph into a list, we end up with this:

The narrative statement should explain:

- What you plan to do and why
- Progress already made
- The relevance of the project to your professional experience
- The significance of this work within your specific and general fields
- Description of specific work plans
- Your goals and the contribution this project will make to the field(s) it engages

Now let's explore (in Table 6.2) how these instructions relate back to the prototypical format we laid out earlier.

TABLE 6.2 Formatting an American Council of Learned Societies Proposal

Prototypical Format		American Council of Learned Societies Proposal Content Guidelines
Introduction/Statement of Problem/ Statement of Purpose	=	What you plan to do and why; your goals
Theoretical Orientation and Significance	=	The significance of this work within your specific and general fields; the contribution this project will make to the field(s) it engages
Methodology/Plan of Work	=	Description of specific work plans
Timeline	=	(Not requested)*
Dissemination of Results	=	(Not requested)*
Qualifications of PI/Team	=	The relevance of the project to your professional experience

* Note that the American Council of Learned Societies does not ask specifically for a project timeline or details of how you will disseminate your results. This does not mean that you can't include these points in your proposal, both of which could logically go under the Description of Specific Work Plans section.

Should you use the verbatim language from the RFP for headers in your proposal? Perhaps, but "What I Plan to Do and Why" does not make for the most elegant header. In this case, you might opt for the headers that we suggest in the prototypical format ("Introduction" or "Statement of Purpose"), or perhaps you would pick up on some of the language from their RFP and name the first section: "Statement of Goals." Then you might call the second section "Theoretical Significance and Contribution." There is no one-size-fits-all solution, except that you must tailor your headers and format in a way that makes sense to the reviewer in tight relation to the RFP and helps guide them effortlessly through your proposal.

The National Science Foundation

d. Project Description (including Results from Prior NSF Support)

(i) Content

The Project Description should provide a clear statement of the work to be undertaken and must include the objectives for the period of the proposed work and expected significance; the relationship of this work to the present state of knowledge in the field, as well as to work in progress by the PI under other support.

The Project Description should outline the general plan of work, including the broad design of activities to be undertaken, and, where appropriate, provide a clear description of experimental methods and procedures. Proposers should address what they want to do, why they want to do it, how they plan to do it, how they will know if they succeed, and what benefits could accrue if the project is successful. The project activities may be based on previously established and/or innovative methods and approaches, but in either case must be well justified. These issues apply to both the technical aspects of the proposal and the way in which the project may make broader contributions.

The National Science Foundation's Proposal and Award Policies and Procedures Guide (PAPPG) is 180 pages chock full of details about writing and submitting your proposal. Only these two excerpted paragraphs provide overall guidance for formulating your project description. However, it is also important to read the current "solicitation" (NSF's term for the RFP) for the individual program—for example, the Cultural Anthropology Program or the Political Science Program—to which you are applying. NSF solicitations provide additional guidance, including a program description that will give you thorough advice about what kinds of topics and projects the program funds. In some cases, these program descriptions will elucidate further instructions or guidance for writing the project description beyond the PAPPG.

Similar to the RFP for the American Council for Learned Societies earlier, the National Science Foundation project description guidance is not crystal clear, leaving some room for interpretation. Using the same exercise that we used earlier, let's first decode the instructions into a potential list of sections and headers:

The project description should provide:

- Objectives for the period of the proposed work and expected significance
- Relation to longer-term goals of the PI's project
- Relation to the present state of knowledge in the field
- Relation to work in progress by the PI under other support
- An outline of the general plan of work, including the broad design of activities to be undertaken
- A clear description of experimental methods and procedures
- What they want to do
- Why they want to do it
- How they plan to do it
- How they will know if they succeed
- What benefits could accrue if the project is successful
- Project activities must be well justified

This list is too long to form the structure of a proposal, and in many cases, the points are repetitive and overlapping. So now, we map these requirements to our prototypical format, although there may be slightly different variations in doing so (Table 6.3).

With an RFP like this, there is no one right answer for choosing header titles, and you must gauge your audience and how they will review your proposal to decide

TABLE 6.3 Formatting a National Science Foundation Proposal

Prototypical Format		National Science Foundation Project Description Guidelines
Introduction/Statement of Problem/Statement of Purpose	=	• Objectives for the period of the proposed work and expected significance
		• What they want to do; why they want to do it
Theoretical Orientation and Significance	=	• Relation to the present state of knowledge in the field
		• Relation to work in progress by the PI under other support
		• What benefits could accrue if the project is successful
Methodology/Plan of Work	=	• Outline of the general plan of work, including the broad design of activities to be undertaken
		• A clear description of experimental methods and procedures
		• How they plan to do it
		• How they will know if they succeed
		• Project activities must be well justified
Timeline	=	(Not requested, but it is advisable to include this)
Dissemination of Results	=	• What benefits could accrue if the project is successful
Qualifications of PI/Team	=	• Relation to longer-term goals of the PI's project

the best language to use. A more extreme example of this is from the Guggenheim Foundation.

The Guggenheim Foundation

A statement of plans for the period for which the Fellowship is requested. Applicants in science or scholarship should provide a detailed, but concise, plan of research, not exceeding three pages in length. Applicants in the arts should submit a brief statement of plans in general terms, not exceeding three pages in length.

This is the only guidance you are going to get from the Guggenheim Foundation. Its simplicity implies that if you are esteemed enough to receive a Guggenheim Fellowship, you better know how to write a good proposal. It also hints at another trend that we see more so with foundation funding than with federal funding: sometimes *who you are* will trump how effective your proposal is. Even with so little guidance and a three-page limit, we still recommend that you use headers and follow the prototypical format listed earlier, or similar.

The dilemma of vague RFP guidance on proposal formatting takes us back to a lesson that we taught you in Chapter 3. When in doubt, find sample successful proposals from your target agency and mimic the formula.

Mind the Review Criteria

Along with deciphering the instructions for writing the project narrative or description, you must also pay close attention to the review criteria. If you cannot find this in the RFP or on the website, contact the program officer. This information gives you extensive insights into how the reviewer will be assessing your proposal. Let's take the review criteria for a National Institutes of Health R01 grant, for example. Reviewers are told explicitly to evaluate, score, and comment on the following criteria:

1. **Significance**: Does the project address an important problem or a critical barrier to progress in the field? If the aims of the project are achieved, how will scientific knowledge, technical capability, and/or clinical practice be improved? How will successful completion of the aims change the concepts, methods, technologies, treatments, services, or preventative interventions that drive this field?

2. **Investigator(s)**: Are the PD/PIs, collaborators, and other researchers well suited to the project? If early stage investigators or new investigators, or in the early stages of independent careers, do they have appropriate experience and training? If established, have they demonstrated an ongoing record of accomplishments that have advanced their field(s)? If the project is collaborative or multi-PD/PI, do the investigators have complementary and integrated expertise; are their leadership approach, governance, and organizational structure appropriate for the project?

3. **Innovation**: Does the application challenge and seek to shift current research or clinical practice paradigms by utilizing novel theoretical concepts, approaches or methodologies, instrumentation, or interventions? Are the concepts, approaches or methodologies, instrumentation, or interventions novel to one field of research or novel in a broad sense? Is a refinement, improvement, or new application of theoretical concepts, approaches or methodologies, instrumentation, or interventions proposed?

4. **Approach**: Are the overall strategy, methodology, and analyses well reasoned and appropriate to accomplish the specific aims of the project? Are potential problems, alternative strategies, and benchmarks for success presented? If the project is in the early stages of development, will the strategy establish feasibility, and will particularly risky aspects be managed? If the project involves clinical research, are the plans for 1) protection of human subjects from research risks and 2) inclusion of minorities and members of both sexes/genders, as well as the inclusion of children, justified in terms of the scientific goals and research strategy proposed?

5. **Environment**: Will the scientific environment in which the work will be done contribute to the probability of success? Are the institutional support, equipment, and other physical resources available to the investigators adequate for the project proposed? Will the project benefit from unique features of the scientific environment, subject populations, or collaborative arrangements?

As this example shows, reviewers are required to consider several details as they review each proposal and are often required to write comments that thoroughly respond to each review criterion. It is your job to make this easy for the reviewers to do. As you write, consciously develop your proposal narrative in a way that answers the criteria and questions that the reviewers will focus on. Provide this information for them, and do not make them have to look for it, or worse, not be able to find it at all. You might even add an extra header and section to address one or more of the review criteria if they do not obviously fit into another section of your proposal. When you have a draft proposal ready for preliminary review, ask your advisor, mentor, colleagues, or Research Development Office to review your proposal with a specific eye toward whether or not you have matched the criteria.

Use Metanarrative

We do not use the term "metanarrative" in the post-modern sense (à la Lyotard). Instead we define it as explanatory language that orients the reader to what they are about to read. The introduction section of your proposal serves as metanarrative for the entire proposal. After the introduction, each section of your proposal should begin with one or two sentences of metanarrative that summarize that section up front. After selecting the best header for each proposal section, metanarrative goes one step further by briefly but clearly orienting the reviewer as they navigate the proposal. The goal is to make the reading easier by giving them a road map of where they are about to go intellectually. Some reviewers frankly do not read in depth more than the first paragraph or two of each proposal section. By including metanarrative you are guaranteeing that the reviewer will take home the key ideas.

Many proposal writers, we have found, feel a strong need to foreground every key point with paragraphs and paragraphs of background information before hitting the reviewer with the main point as a sort of grand finale to each section or indeed the entire proposal. Although this may lead to a magnificent revelatory experience for the reviewer, you are assuming that the reviewer will get that far. More likely is that she will give up halfway in, wondering when you are going to get to the point. Even if it feels unnatural, and even if you fear that the reviewer won't "get it," you should begin each section with a metanarrative summary of the main point and then proceed with filling in the background, substance, and details. Do not bury your main points in the middle or end of the proposal and its sections if you want them to be read. We will provide examples of effective metanarrative in later chapters when we analyze sections of successful HSS proposals.

To Use or Not to Use Jargon

Many agencies and RFPs speak directly to this question, with statements such as "Please avoid discipline-specific jargon that may pose a problem for non-specialists" (American Council of Learned Societies RFP). This warning is given because agencies often send proposals to nonspecialist reviewers in at least one phase of the review process. You do not want to alienate a reviewer under any circumstances. Reading a proposal that is dense with jargon is off-putting, even for those who understand it.

At the same time, it might be difficult in some cases to talk about important points of your project without using jargon that is specific to your subfield. You do not want specialist reviewers to think that you don't know Foucault's "panopticon" metaphor, for example, if it plays a major role in your analysis. Particularly in emerging fields, such as digital humanities, scholars are actively inventing and engaging in new concepts and language that play a large role in cutting-edge research. If you are seeking to understand how emerging technologies are transforming the human experience, for instance, you cannot get around using the shorthand phrase "augmented reality," which is accepted in digital humanities scholarship and thinking. Therefore, in these cases you should use an important word or phrase that is jargony, but follow it up with a brief definition or explanation. Just make sure to vet your proposal with preliminary reviewers from other disciplines (your advisor's husband from the department on the other side of campus, members of your online writing group, etc.) and ask them specifically to tell you if it is understandable.

Be Convincing and Do Not Introduce Doubt

As the adage attributed to Einstein goes, "If we knew what it was we were doing, it wouldn't be called 'research,' would it?" But program officers want to know that you are a good bet. They do not want to write a check for $100,000 to someone who isn't quite sure what he is doing. To this point, avoid words such as "if," "should," "might," "would," "try," "perhaps," "hope." Replace them with definitive words such as "when," "will," "shall," "expect," etc. These are some of the little white lies of proposal writing.

It goes without saying that you should do as much preliminary research about your topic as possible. But if you don't have a seed grant, or a loan from your parents, to visit potential field sites or conduct a pilot study, it may be necessary to "wing it" in certain areas of your proposal. Do as much due diligence as possible, even if that means searching the Internet and making international phone calls to identify the optimal village in Ethiopia to study the effects of fair trade coffee marketing on African farmers.

Then, once you have settled on your best estimate, write about it as if it is truth. You should not trouble the reviewers with this small uncertainty by explaining that you will need to do further inquiries before settling on the finer points of the work plan. For the purposes of the proposal, pick one Ethiopian village for now and run with it. If you get the money, you can work out the details later. But you will not get the money if you reveal that you are several small steps shy of a definite plan.

Conveying the appearance of certainty by glossing over tentative areas of your research only applies to the smaller details that will not affect the overall scope and theoretical contributions one way or the other. For example, if you propose to do research in Taiwan, but later decide that Honduras is a better fit, this will give a program officer pause when you request permission to change the scope of work. In any case, there is only so much "little white lying" that you can do in a proposal before it is obvious that you are not ready to do your research.

Having said that, there are some important instances when you should discuss potential pitfalls and contingency plans, such as in the case of exploratory or high-risk research that could not, by design, pan out as intended. The National Institutes of Health, for example, explicitly asks for this information in a proposal. As such, you must identify and describe the risks and probabilities, along with clear and convincing options for alternative experiments or methods in the event that Plan A goes awry. To be convincing about doing this kind of research, you will typically need to have an established reputation and track record in your field, and the potential benefits of the risky research must be compelling.

Writing 101—Some Writing Basics

We end this chapter with a roundup of the most common mistakes and glitches that we see when we review proposals:

- You *must* follow the guidelines. Particularly for federal agencies, we are seeing more and more proposals returned without review for the smallest infractions in the rules (such as a biographical sketch being formatted incorrectly for the National Science Foundation).
- Follow the agency guidelines regarding margins, line spacing, and font size. If they do not provide guidelines, then use *at least* 10-point font, 1-inch margins, and as much white space as possible on a page.
- Clarity in thought and writing is paramount in research proposals. If you know that you are not a good writer, take a course or hire a good copy editor to help you with your proposal.
- Keep sentences short and focused on a single point. A common rule of thumb is to keep a sentence to twenty words or less. Proposals are not the place for sentences with multiple independent clauses.
- Use first-person pronouns (I or we if a collaborative proposal), and the active, as opposed to the passive, voice. For instance, write: "I will conduct participant observation in the factory" not "Participant observation in the factory will be conducted."
- The word "data" is the plural form. Make sure to have subject–verb agreement when talking about data, as in "The data **are** . . ."
- A certain amount of redundancy in a proposal is good. Don't be shy about artfully repeating main points throughout your proposal, especially if it is ten or more pages. By the time a reviewer arrives at the methods section on page seven, the research questions from page one might be a distant memory.

- Use figures, diagrams, tables, or infographics to convey complex ideas or connections between components of your research project. Make sure that they communicate and simplify effectively, instead of adding to the confusion. Use them sparingly, and make sure that they can be understood in black and white.
- Consider using boldface, underlining, or bullets to draw attention to essential words, phrases, or small sections of your proposal. If you decide to use these devices, use them prudently. It is vexing to a reviewer to see boldface words and sentences in every paragraph. This kind of highlighting should be reserved for main points that might otherwise be buried. Using effective metanarrative and front-loading your main ideas will preclude having to call out important information in the rest of the proposal.

Summary

This chapter illustrates that a proposal is a careful balancing act. It must convey your rigorous research as clearly as possible, while simultaneously addressing the multiple requirements of the request for proposals and review criteria, and keeping your reviewer riveted. There are several ways to keep your reader tuned in as they read the proposal; in particular, use headers, use metanarrative, and mirror the RFP and review criteria. Always keep your audience in mind when writing, and give them what they are looking for.

Now that you have an overview of how to format and structure your proposal, we will spend the next three chapters of this book walking you through writing the main substantive sections of your proposal. These consist of:

- Introduction/Statement of Problem/Statement of Purpose
- Theoretical Orientation/Framework and Significance
- Methodology/Procedures/Plan of Work

After those, we go on to provide you with tips and resources for writing the remaining sections of your proposal, including the budget and budget justification, the timeline, the dissemination plan, the qualifications of the PI, letters of recommendation, the bibliography, and appendices.

BOX 6.1 FLASH TOPIC: FREEWRITING

Writer's block? Can't find your writing mojo? Paralyzed by a section of your proposal?

We say forget about it and just write!

Along with a daily writing practice that we describe in Chapter 4, your overall writing productivity and prowess will benefit from freewriting. Freewriting is a method developed by Peter Elbow, who experienced his own battles with writing, which led to this technique. As described in his book *Writing Without Teachers* (New York: Oxford UP, 1973),

> the idea is simply to write for ten minutes (later on, perhaps fifteen or twenty). Don't stop for anything. Go quickly without rushing. Never stop to look back, to cross something out, to wonder how to spell something, to wonder what word or thought to use, or to think about what you are doing. If you can't think of a word or a spelling, just use a squiggle or else write "I can't think what to say, I can't think what to say" as many times as you want; or repeat the last word you wrote over and over again; or anything else. The only requirement is that you never stop.

As Elbow goes on to say, "Freewriting may seem crazy but actually it makes simple sense." Especially when you are "stuck," freewriting will help get you through it and on to productive writing. The mantra is "write now, edit later." Don't get bogged down with "getting it right" in perfectly erudite and grammatically correct sentences. Just get your ideas on paper—even if they are confusing, half-formed, or just plain bad—and organize them later.

The act of freewriting can also help you identify why you are stuck. Dr. Karen Lunsford, Professor of Writing at UC Santa Barbara, offers several prompts to give your proposal freewriting some direction. Instead of writing what you are supposed to be writing, try writing *about* what you are supposed to be writing or why you can't write. Try these prompts:

- What questions do I want to answer in my research?
- What trends am I seeing in my theoretical review?
- What do I want to accomplish next?
- I am stuck on this section. Why?

Writing about your writing (or lack thereof) can help solve knotty problems in the conceptualization of your research proposal. By exploring your frustration with your proposal writing and proposal sections, you may identify some larger problems in your research design. For example, perhaps you are trying to tie together too many disparate theoretical strands. Perhaps your methodology can't answer your research questions. Perhaps you don't know enough about aspects of your research design to write about them convincingly. The insights you gain from freewriting are known to get your writing back on track!

For more information about Elbow's "freewriting," see his publications:

Elbow, P. (1998). *Writing Without Teachers*. New York: Oxford University Press.

Elbow, P. (1998). *Writing With Power: Techniques for Mastering the Writing Process*. New York: Oxford University Press.

Elbow, P. (1989). Toward a phenomenology of freewriting. *Journal of Basic Writing, 8*(2), 42–71.

Note

1 We focus here on only a very small part of the RFPs. We urge you to read the RFPs in their entirety to learn about all the expectations for your proposal, such as font size, line spacing, additional documents to include, etc.

7

WRITING THE INTRODUCTION/ STATEMENT OF PROBLEM/ STATEMENT OF PURPOSE

First impressions count, and the introduction section of your proposal must be terrific. Depending on the length of your proposal, the introduction should be between one paragraph and one page long. Regardless of the length, you must use the opportunity to concisely "frame" your proposal for the reviewer and orient them to what they are about to read. Do not make a reviewer wait until page 2 or 3 to find out what the proposal is about. As we have mentioned before, proposal writing does not follow murder mystery plot development. Put the main point up front, or you will immediately lose the interest and patience of your reviewer.

Framing

By framing we mean that you need to contextualize your research project in the relevant literature, state your research question(s) or objective(s), and explain what you expect to find out and why it will make a significant contribution. Here, you might also allude to the other components of your proposal such as the methods, timeline, and other benefits of the research results. This sounds like a lot of information to pack into the introduction, but here we show you a pattern for assembling this information in the most compelling way.[1]

Framing is a device by which *you* control how your proposal is read by reviewers. If we imagine proposal writing as a contact sport, framing allows you to:

- Draw the lines on the playing field
- Choose the players
- Choose the ball
- Create the rules
- Fix the final results of the game

Successful framing will lead the reviewers inevitably through the process of under-standing and interpreting your research in a specific and strategic way. Framing devices are used throughout the proposal, but framing must begin with the very first sentence.

The "Hook"

Before we describe our pattern for introductions, we want to briefly discuss a widely advised and used strategy for kicking off a research proposal. Many scholars swear by the "hook": a catchy anecdote, a news headline, or a startling statistic to capture the reader's attention. Others begin with a provocative question or a pithy epigraph to set the theme. We encourage you to try out these strategies within the pattern we lay out next, but do not cross the line over into cute or gratuitous gimmick. This type of writing "move" must be relevant and insightful in relation to the proposal and not just a ploy to make an otherwise lackluster proposal memorable.

As explained in Chapters 5 and 6, you cannot write your proposal without first knowing the relevant literature and how your research project fits into and contributes to it. The first several sentences in your proposal should establish this information for the reviewer. We suggest a step-by-step recipe for organizing this information, as follows:

1. Common knowledge: existing or status quo knowledge in your field
2. Disruptor: gaps or problems in the existing literature, destabilizing information that questions common knowledge
3. Research question(s)
4. Hypothesis or expectations
5. Why the research is significant
6. Mention of the plan of work and methods

This is a common and logical pattern for introductions, and once you become familiar with it, you will realize that many proposals and research articles begin this way. In fact, you may already be writing your introductions this way. This is not to say that every funded proposal follows this introduction pattern to a tee, and it is not the only option that will be successful. Nevertheless, we urge you to learn this pattern, apply it to your research proposal writing, and then explore different ways of altering it depending on the particulars of your project and the funding opportunity. Especially if you are just starting to think about your research project, following this recipe will take you through the steps of clarifying your project and its significance in your own mind.

Common Knowledge

Your first couple of sentences should summarize the current common conceptions held by those who work in your research area, or the public. These sentences dem-onstrate your understanding of the existing literature, set up the context for your contribution, and orient the reader to the "playing field" as described earlier. You must judge how narrow or wide the framing should be, and you should decide this based on who the likely reviewers will be. If you know that your review panel will be composed of a multidisciplinary panel of scholars or a foundation board of non-academics, then keep this information broad and understandable to the nonspecialist. If you know that your reviewers will be scholars in your same subfield, then you can begin to frame your project at a higher resolution with the more specific literature and language that you will engage theoretically. It is typical to find citations after each of these sentences.

Disruptor

After establishing the common knowledge, you should immediately insert a disruptor. These next sentences summarize the research problem or what is missing or inconsistent about the common conceptions of the field. They should explain, for example, what has not been adequately addressed or unresolved questions or debates. These sentences expose the gap in the existing literature or common understanding and begin to tell the story of how your research will make a contribution. The transition from the common knowledge to the disruptor is marked by predictable words, such as "still," "but," "yet," "although," "nevertheless," "however," "less is known about," etc.

Research Question(s)

After setting up the research problem through the common knowledge–disruptor pattern, the stage is set to introduce the research questions by which you will solve the identified problem, gap, inconsistency, etc. We believe that every proposal should state an overarching question or set of questions that guides your research project. They should be stated as questions.

We see many proposals that fall short of asking definitive research questions, such as "topics to explore" or "areas of interest." These kinds of vague statements can lead a reviewer to wonder if you have a concrete research plan. By the time you are asking for money for a project, it should be boiled down to a tight argument that leaves little room for doubt about what you are going to do. Your research questions might also be accompanied by aims or objectives.

Keep the number of research questions to a minimum. For a typical project, four research questions is the absolute maximum. If you have more than three questions, they should be interrelated or nested. And as emphasized in prior chapters, these questions must be of a theoretical nature, related to how your new data or analysis of materials will transform your scholarly area or discipline. This is not the place to explain what questions you will ask informants in interviews and focus groups, for example. As mentioned throughout this book, proposal writing is an exercise in editing your thoughts and reducing complexity to something that is conceptually manageable by haggard reviewers. There is only so much you can accomplish in a research project, particularly if the funding is limited to one year or less. So boil down your myriad questions to a couple of essential questions that will get you the most mileage toward a coherent proposal.

Hypothesis or Expectations

Logically following your research questions, you should next explain what you expect to find in your research. Some might call these hypotheses. Others might less scientifically say "I anticipate finding that . . ." Your discipline will dictate whether your research should have formal hypotheses or not. But regardless of what you call them or how detailed they are, you should absolutely have a sense of what kinds of things you expect to find in your project. This does not mean that your project must necessarily be "thesis driven" or that the results are a foregone conclusion. After all, you are doing research and you still need to collect and analyze your data or materials.

A compelling research proposal conveys that you are an expert in your field and that you know enough about your topic to anticipate at least broad, if not specific, outcomes of the research activities. In fact, some agencies will only fund research if there are preliminary data or pilot research that shows "proof of concept" for your larger project. If you are clueless about the potential results of your research, and thus your contribution to the field, then you will not be able to present a good case for funding your project. If you are in this position, look for a seed grant to do exploratory work, or do independent preliminary research to gain more insights into your topic.

Why the Research Is Significant

Your introduction should also explain the significance of the research. What are the benefits of your project? What new things will we know? What theoretical advances will be made? What are the costs of not finding out this information? Be explicit about this. Do not allow the reviewers to deduce this on their own. Although the significance may seem obvious to you, do not leave room for doubt or misunderstanding among the reviewers.

Allude to Plan of Work and Methods

At some point in the introduction, you should briefly mention your plan of work and possibly your methods. If you are asking for a year of funding to write your book, let this be known from the beginning of your proposal. If you want funding to do three years of fieldwork, mention it up front. And space permitting, refer to your methods in a general way.

All of these elements together set the stage for your project. Again, they are:

1. Common knowledge
2. Disruptor

3. Research question(s)
4. Hypothesis or expectations
5. Why the research is significant
6. Mention of the plan of work and methods

By the end of the first page of your proposal, if written concisely in this pattern, the reviewer knows exactly what is about to happen. They are not confused. They are not holding on to different threads in their head wondering how they will all come together. They have enough information to be intrigued and excited to see how the details play out in the rest of the proposal.

Introduction Examples Decoded

Next we decode and annotate two introduction sections of successful proposals from HSS disciplines. For each excerpt, we have identified the different components to the passage (Common Knowledge, Disruptor Research Question, Hypothesis/Expectations, Significance, and Plan of Work/Methods). They may not contain all of the components, and they may not follow our prescribed sequence of the components perfectly. As you study these, consider how you can adapt your research ideas to our introduction formula.

BOX 7.1 PROPOSAL EXCERPT: INTRODUCTION FROM A PROPOSAL FOR THE AMERICAN COUNCIL OF LEARNED SOCIETIES BURKHARDT FELLOWSHIP

Title: Diet for a Warm Planet: Debating the Future Map of Food

Author: Susanne Freidberg, PhD, Geography

This proposal effectively has two pairs of the common knowledge–disruptor pattern. The first begins with an anecdote that draws the reviewer in to the substantive topic through a discussion about a pizzeria menu. This strategy connects a common everyday experience to the substantive topic of the proposal and includes a disruptor to set the stage for the scholarly problem and questions posed in the proposal. We consider this an exemplary use of "the hook."

A new pizzeria has just opened in my neighborhood, offering "local, organic and sustainable food." In boldface the menu asks "Did you know that the average bite of American food travels more than 1,500 miles before it reaches your lips?" It would be hard not to know by now, as this factoid has become both ubiquitous and oddly self-explanatory. "Which is why," the menu continues, "we do business with 30 farms and businesses throughout New England." Presumably those farms don't supply the olives and anchovies.

Common Knowledge

Their proximity, however, implies food that is better for consumers, the local economy, and the global environment.

Disruptor

Over the past few years, mounting concerns about climate change have fortified already vigorous local food movements, especially in the United States and Britain. Initiatives to encourage relocalization have won government and corporate support.

Common Knowledge

Yet the climatic arguments for bringing food "back home" are less clear-cut than the pizzeria's menu would suggest, especially when weighed against the potential harm to developing countries' agro-exporters. The seemingly technical question of how to measure food's footprint has become part of the broader debate over how and where to define the borders of a sustainable diet.

Disruptor

How is this debate over the future map of food supply also a struggle over the kinds of expert knowledge used to draw it?

Research Question

A Burkhardt Fellowship will provide the time, resources, and interdisciplinary setting needed to address this question. A year in residence at the Radcliffe Institute of Advanced Studies will give me access not only to the institute's own diverse group of fellows, but also to materials and scholars located in the Boston-Cambridge area. These include the Harvard library system, especially the Schlesinger Library's culinary collection; the science and technology studies (STS) programs at both Harvard and MIT; and the many scientists and engineers working in fields related to climate change and sustainability. The latter will count among my ethnographic subjects in a long-term project incorporating the insights of STS, cultural geography, and food studies.

Mention of Work Plan and Methods

This project will advance humanities scholarship that explores the claims we make about the natural world, especially as a source of nourishment. It will also shed a timely light on the history, epistemologies, and power relations informing contemporary discussions about where food should come from.

Significance

BOX 7.2 PROPOSAL EXCERPT: INTRODUCTION FROM A PROPOSAL FOR THE NATIONAL SCIENCE FOUNDATION DOCTORAL DISSERTATION IMPROVEMENT GRANT

Title: The Politics of War Trauma: A Case Study of St. Elizabeth's Hospital, 1890–1930

Author: Moira O'Neil, PhD, Sociology

This is a proposal for sociological research that takes a qualitative methodological approach. The author has used bullets to denote the research questions, which we think is an excellent way to make sure they are easy to find for the reviewer, especially for longer proposals.

From the Civil War-era "soldier's heart" to post-Vietnam's Post-traumatic Stress Disorder (PTSD), shifts in diagnoses and treatment of the psychological impacts of war in the United States are a rich site to examine the cultural, political, and economic determinants of psychiatric classification and practice.	**Common Knowledge**
The medicalization of war trauma in the U.S. prior to the formal recognition of the PTSD diagnosis in 1980, however, remains understudied. Scholarship on Britain, Germany and France has demonstrated that state policy around disability pensions for veterans, psychiatrists' relationship to state policy objectives, and discursive constructions of soldiers' social identity were critical determinants of the medicalization of war-related mental illness at the beginning of the twentieth century (Bourke 1996; Leese 2002; Lerner 2003; Showalter 1985).	**Disruptor**

Informed by these comparative cases in Western Europe, this dissertation is an in-depth case study of the diagnosis and treatment of "insane soldiers" institutionalized at St. Elizabeth's Hospital in Washington D.C. from 1890 to 1930.

Significance

It addresses the following research questions:

Research Questions

- What was the impact of pensions for soldiers with psychological disabilities on the medicalization of war trauma in the U.S.?

- Within St. Elizabeth's, what assumptions about nonnormative psychological responses to warfare authorized the production of "war neurosis" and how did those assumptions shift over time?

- Who were the soldiers institutionalized at St. Elizabeth's and how did they construct their experience of war-related mental illness?

To address these questions, this dissertation draws on three types of archival data generated between 1890 and 1930 that are housed at the *National Archives* and the *Library of Congress* in Washington D.C.: (1) patient registry and medical files of soldiers institutionalized at St. Elizabeth's; (2) administrative records from this hospital; (3) and legislative records and veterans' advocacy materials regarding the formation of social policy for psychologically injured soldiers. The patient registry will be analyzed to create profiles of typical military admissions to St. Elizabeth's and provide a sampling frame for in-depth analysis of soldiers' medical files. The remaining archival data will be analyzed as qualitative texts following the extended case method (Burawoy 1998).

Mention of Work Plan and Methods

The findings will explicate the role
of state policy, and specifically
disability pensions for soldiers,
in shaping diagnostic categories
and therapeutic regimens for war-
related mental illness; analyze the
institutional production of medical
knowledge about the psychological
effects of war at St. Elizabeth's
Hospital; and finally, examine the
ways in which soldiers made sense of,
challenged and consented to dominant
medical and political notions of their
war experience. This in-depth case
will lay the groundwork for cross-case
theorizing with research on Britain,
Germany and France during this period.

Significance

Summary

In this chapter, we have provided a formula for writing the proposal introduction. Whether you are just beginning to conceptualize your next research project or are attempting to rewrite a rejected proposal, using this formula can help you sort through your key research questions and why they are significant. Although your final product may not end up looking exactly like our suggested recipe, using this heuristic to think through the introduction can at least be a generative writing exercise that enables you to establish a solid foundation for the proposal. In sum, remember that the introduction sets the stage for the reviewer. It is your job to "frame" the proposal from the very first sentence in a way that sets you up for success. Using the common knowledge–disruptor pattern will make the scholarly significance of your research stand out immediately. By following our suggested formula, everything the reviewer needs to know is easy to find and in a logical order.

In the next chapter, we explore rhetorical strategies for the Theoretical or Conceptual Framework section of the proposal. As you will soon see, this section also follows the common knowledge–disruptor pattern in a longer form.

BOX 7.3 INTRODUCTION EXERCISE

1. Find two successful proposals (search online or ask peers and mentors).
2. Find two unsuccessful proposals (ask peers and mentors or perhaps look back at some of your own unsuccessful attempts).

3. Analyze the Introduction sections of these proposals.
   a. Is there a distinct Introduction section?
   b. Does the Introduction have a common knowledge–disruptor pattern?
   c. Can you easily identify the research question(s)?
   d. Is there a hypothesis(es) or anticipated outcomes?
   e. Are the methods and plan of work mentioned?
   f. Can you clearly understand what the proposal entails by the end of the first page?
   g. Can you clearly understand the significance of the research by the end of the Introduction section?
4. Compare the successful proposals against the unsuccessful proposals. What similarities and differences do you find?

Note

1 We are indebted to Professor Karen Lunsford of the Writing Program at UC Santa Barbara and Barbara Herr Harthorn of the Department of Anthropology at UC Santa Barbara for sharing their approaches to, and materials for, writing introductions during several years of co-teaching proposal writing workshops and seminars with us. The approach we teach here is based on their proposal writing paradigms, as well as the Little Red Schoolhouse curricula, originally conceived at the University of Chicago by Joe Williams, Greg Colomb, Frank Kinahan, and Peter Blaney. More information about it can be found here: http://writing-program.uchicago.edu/courses/.

8

WRITING THE THEORETICAL ORIENTATION AND SIGNIFICANCE SECTION

The theoretical significance of your project is instrumental to the success of your proposal. This is the main intellectual factor by which your proposal is judged. Therefore, it should be the central theme around which you build your proposal, and every other proposal component will follow from it. The Theoretical Orientation and Significance section is *not* a literature review. The focus is less on the relevant literature and more on how you will be making an exciting contribution to it. Therefore, you must be explicit throughout this section as to how *your* proposed project will add to the literature that you review.

The depth and level of your discussion of the relevant theoretical literature should be targeted toward the anticipated review panel. If the review panel is multidisciplinary, you might have to start at a low resolution and explain some of the more general, fundamental antecedents to your work. If you know your reviewers will be more specialized in your area of expertise, you can begin at a level that is much further downstream in your scholarly argument. But remember, it is less likely that your proposal will be read only by specialists in your micro-field. Even if they are the first readers, you cannot expect them to explain and defend your impenetrable proposal to the next round of interdisciplinary panel reviewers.

It is important in the Theoretical Orientation and Significance section to edit and narrow your ideas to a limited amount of information. Your project may have implications for several theoretical areas, but you need to decide which are the most compelling and will resonate most with the reviewers. There is not a formula for how much of the literature you should review, because it will depend on the idiosyncrasies of your project. But generally you should aim to discuss up to four theoretical areas in a long proposal, fewer in a short proposal. For each area of theory that you discuss, explicitly describe its current state, its limitations, and how your research:

- Fills the gaps that you identify
- Advances knowledge beyond the existing understandings

- Bridges debates or divergences among the authors that you cite
- Reconsiders current paradigms in your field
- Examines new conditions that call earlier findings into question

Do not assume that the reviewers will make the connections between the literature that you review and your research project. You must clearly and plainly spell it out for them, even if it seems quite obvious to you. Graduate students and junior faculty members may feel somewhat self-conscious about tooting their horn in this way. But proposal writing is not the time to be vague or overly modest. Be reasonable, but be forthcoming about your contributions.

On the other hand, you might feel quite confident about your contributions, and in fact, you might be wondering, "What if I am critical of the existing literature, and I have designed my project to impale and eviscerate every scholarly argument that has come before mine?" In this case our advice is to tone your rhetoric way down, because it is very likely that your reviewers (or their friends) will be among the scholars you critique. Instead of claiming to turn accepted theory "on its head," you want to use milder, respectful language, such as "build on," "shed new light on," "examine through a new lens," and so forth. You should never set out to insult or lambast other scholars to make your contribution seem more compelling.

The Theoretical Orientation and Significance section should begin with a sentence or two that neatly summarizes the entire section. This "metanarrative" will make the reading easier for the reviewer. For example, it should read something along the lines of: "This project engages and builds on three overlapping theoretical fields: economic development, climate change risk perception, and vulnerability and resilience studies." Then, depending on the proposal length, devote one or more paragraphs to your review of and contribution to these three fields.

Each of these paragraphs or subsections should be arranged in similar fashion to the proposal introduction as described in Chapter 7:

1. Common knowledge (what is known)
2. Disruptor (what is not known)
3. Explanation of how your project will contribute

Don't forget that the focus is on *your* project and its significance. Each section should end with a summary statement about how your research will add value. These particular sentences where you spell out your contribution to each field might be a good place to use boldface type, as suggested in Chapter 6. You do not want this information to escape the notice of the reviewer.

Citations and References

The Theoretical Orientation and Significance section is where you often see the most references in a proposal. For the most part, you should cite the existing literature that you discuss and use references. The bibliography should list all the references in your proposal and should not include any others. This becomes challenging when there are restrictive page limits, and you will have to judiciously decide who to leave in and out of your discussion. However, do not neglect to cite the most prominent scholars and articles in your field.

In certain shorter proposals, we have seen successful examples that do not cite other literature specifically, but instead refer more generally to current understandings in the field. These include Guggenheim and National Endowment for the Humanities fellowships, for example. However, as a graduate student or junior faculty member, we do not recommend this cavalier approach in proposal writing. As a novice scholar and proposal writer, the reviewers may be suspicious of your training if you do not cite anyone. They may also be insulted that you have not acknowledged those who have established the foundation for your work. If you question whether and how much to use references in your proposal, find some sample successful proposals from the agency to identify patterns and/or call the program officer to ask for recommendations about best practices.

Theoretical Orientation and Significance Section Examples Decoded

Next we decode two Theoretical Orientation and Significance sections of successful proposals from across the HSS disciplines. For each excerpt, we identify the common knowledge–disruptor pattern and contribution. As mentioned throughout this book, not every successful sample contains all of the components, and they may not follow our prescribed formula. But you can use our prescription as a heuristic until you develop an effective style of your own.

BOX 8.1 PROPOSAL EXCERPT: THEORETICAL ORIENTATION AND SIGNIFICANCE SECTION FROM A PROPOSAL TO THE GUGGENHEIM FOUNDATION FELLOWSHIP PROGRAM

Title: Revelatory Events: Otherworldly Experiences and New Visionary Movements

Author: Ann Taves, PhD, Religious Studies

This excerpt is from a three-page proposal, for which the agency gives very little guidance. The author chose her own section header titles and organized the Theoretical Orientation and Significance section around three main areas of research: a) religious studies, b) creativity studies, and c) research on new religious movements within the behavioral sciences. As you will see in the analysis, she treats each theoretical area separately, explicitly providing the common knowledge–disruptor pattern and her contribution to each. She gives more attention to the third theme, as this is the main significance of the research. You will also notice that in the third theme, the pattern is slightly altered. Here, the author starts with a disrupting sentence, as opposed to common knowledge, but this information follows shortly.

The proposal is targeted to a specialized audience, and the author assumed that the Guggenheim Foundation would send the proposal to reviewers in her subfields. As you can see, the proposal also uses a good amount of specialized language, or "jargon," although she takes the time to define certain concepts and terms that may be less familiar to her intended audience. Here is the way that we have decoded this proposal section into the crucial elements:

Theoretical Contributions: This project will make a significant contribution to three fields: religious studies, creativity studies, and research on new religious movements within the behavioral sciences.	**Metanarrative**
Within religious studies, scholars typically begin by stipulating a definition of religion.	**Common Knowledge for Theoretical Area 1 (religious studies)**
Doing so, however, limits our ability to examine the processes of interpretation through which people decide whether events, experiences, or cultural products are religious or not (Taves 2011).	**Disruptor for Theoretical Area 1**
This project examines cases in which both the experiences and their results are hard to categorize in order to develop a method of analysis that does not obscure the interpretive processes it seeks to explore.	**Contribution for Theoretical Area 1**
Research on creativity (Weisberg 2006, Kaufman and Sternberg 2010) discusses innovation in the realms of science, technology, business, literature, and the arts	**Common Knowledge for Theoretical Area 2 (creativity studies)**
but rarely mentions religion.	**Disruptor for Theoretical Area 2**
In interpreting revelatory claims as a product of creative small group processes, I treat them as a type of innovation, while at the same time identifying and explaining the competing assumptions that often lead subjects to reject this comparison.	**Contribution for Theoretical Area 2**

Within the behavioral sciences, theoretical models have not adequately explored the effects of unusual individual abilities (real or perceived) on small group processes nor considered the role of group interpretations of unusual experiences in shaping what emerges.

Disruptor for Theoretical Area 3 (new religious movements within the behavioral sciences)

By analyzing a diverse set of cases from the perspective of the cognitive social sciences (Sun 2012), this study offers a more unified approach.

Contribution for Theoretical Area 3

State of the Field: Within the behavioral sciences, three theories are particularly relevant for understanding the underlying psychosocial dynamics: Max Weber's theoretical work on prophets and charismatic authority (1956), Anthony Wallace's theory of revitalization movements (1956), and Rodney Stark's sociological theory of revelation (1999). Each of these theories has its strengths. Weber highlights the role of followers in the making of charismatic leaders, Wallace highlights the role of visionary experiences in promoting cognitive transformations ("mazeway resynthesis") that lead to cultural revitalization, and Stark highlights the role of intense primary groups in the emergence of new revelation.

Common Knowledge for Theoretical Area 3

Although each contributes something to our understanding of the dynamics, their insights need to be integrated in light of more recent multilevel interactive models (Thagard 2012) that neither reduce the social to the psychological nor individuals to socio-cultural constructions. Crucially, none devotes sufficient attention to the process of interpretation and decision-making as it unfolds from the point of view of the people involved with the emergent movement, whether as supporters or critics. Insufficient attention to the interplay between these factors leaves theorists unable to relate diverse, culturally specific outcomes to the more generic underlying dynamics.

Disruptor for Theoretical Area 3

Utilizing process-tracing methods, i.e., historical methods adapted by social scientists to analyze case studies and generate theories (George & Bennett 2005), this project demonstrates how interpretation and decision-making processes channel psycho-social dynamics to generate diverse cultural products that take various social forms.

Contribution for Theoretical Area 3

Main Point: Drawing in particular on Stark's insight that small intimate face-to-face groups play a crucial role in the interpretation and elaboration of unusual experiences, I argue that both the interactions of the group and the outcomes of their interaction depend to a significant extent on the form, the content, and the elaboration of the unusual experience—that is, on what interacting subjects view as emerging and how they decide to act on it. Experiences and psychosocial processes that have some underlying features in common can unfold in a variety of ways depending on the content of the unusual experience and the way interlocutors react as the process unfolds. While there is no one path or product, we can nonetheless analyze the way the process unfolds over time as the interlocutors encounter, choose, explain, and transmit new consensual realities that carry real life consequences for those who participate in them.

BOX 8.2   PROPOSAL EXCERPT: THEORETICAL ORIENTATION AND SIGNIFICANCE SECTION FROM A PROPOSAL TO THE NATIONAL SCIENCE FOUNDATION

Title: New Indian Wars: The Challenge of Indigenous Sovereignty

Author: Eve Darian-Smith, PhD, Anthropology

This excerpt is from a proposal that was funded by the Law and Social Sciences Program at the National Science Foundation. The proposal length is fifteen pages for a regular grant. This gives the author ample space to make a thorough argument about the theoretical context and significance of the proposed research. After reviewing and discussing her contribution to each of her theoretical areas, she takes the extra step to sum up all of her contributions in a separate proposal section specifically titled "Intellectual Merit." Intellectual merit is one of two main review criteria at the National Science Foundation (along with broader impacts). By using this header in her proposal, she is calling inescapable attention to the essential theoretical and scholarly merits of the project that the reviewer will be looking for.

THEORETICAL AND HISTORICAL BACKGROUND OF THE PROPOSED RESEARCH	**Metanarrative**
This research will address three areas of scholarship: a) critical race theory; b) shifting conceptualizations of indigenous sovereignty and the ways these understandings inform the legal field; and c) analyses of Indian gaming and its impact on the economic, political and social landscape of US racial politics, especially as it pertains to Native Americans. Together these three fields complement and deepen existing work conducted within critical race scholarship that typically overlooks native issues, as well as understandings of the linked constitution of evolving legal concepts and dynamic socio-cultural identities.	
(1) Critical race theory	**Common Knowledge for Theoretical Area 1** (critical race theory)
One of the common accusations against Native Americans is that they represent "special interests" and receive special legal rights that allow them to install gaming operations on reservation land. It is the fact of reservation land, and the sovereign control over such land by tribal governments, that legally entitles tribes to erect casinos where non-Indians cannot.	

What is often forgotten in the bitter accusations of special entitlement is that reservation land is emblematic of past colonial injustices and federal polices of exploitation as practiced under the Indian Removal Act of 1830. This act allowed the forcible removal of tens of thousands of Cherokee, Seminoles, Choctaws and other native groups from Georgia and other southern states, and forced the migration of native peoples westward. Over the subsequent decades, reservation communities became targets of further exploitation and violence, with Indian lands broken up under the Dawes Act of 1887 and the federal responsibility under treaty negotiations to provide social services denied (Wilkins 2008; Darian-Smith 2010a:180-208).

Disruptor for Theoretical Area 1

The current racialization of "rich Indians" as undeserving beneficiaries of new rules allowing for gaming operations is the latest iteration of a long history of legal manipulation and legally endorsed violence directed against native peoples. But it is also an instance of a different set of historical patterns that have traditionally not involved impoverished native communities.

As critical race theorists have argued, economic success by underprivileged people has historically triggered racism by their oppressors. A history of resentment toward economically successful ex-slaves after emancipation (Litwack 1980), blacks in the reconstruction era (Foner 2002), Irish Catholics in the second half of the 19th century (Casey and Lee 2007), Japanese immigrants in California (Chan 1991; Azuma 2005), Korean shop-keepers in

Common Knowledge for Theoretical Area 1

major US cities (Light and Bonacich 1991; Chang 1993; Ancheta 2006), and so on suggest that the burgeoning resentment against casino-owning Native Americans is a new configuration of these political and cultural responses to economic prosperity. In short, the proposed research is situated within wider debates on citizenship and race in US society, and a long history of resentment against economic competition and success from people of color in the context of a dominant white culture.

However, thinking about indigenous rights from the perspective of critical race theory and as an issue of racial justice is not the norm in the United States. To date, Native Americans have not featured in scholarship on the connection between racism and socio-economic success, which has typically been framed by either black/white race relations (Crenshaw 1996; Delgado and Stefancic 2001), or debates over immigration and new citizenship (Park 2004). A speaker series in 2010 at UCLA law school sought to explore this disconnect, declaring "Native peoples' experiences with race and racism are usually invisible. Tribal efforts to assert sovereignty, where visible, are not usually framed as struggles for racial justice."

Disruptor for Theoretical Area 1

This proposed research seeks to situate conflict over the concept of indigenous sovereignty firmly within the theoretical insights of critical race theory, and explore the underlying and deeply embedded racialized rhetoric, imagery, assumptions, and identities that accompany the use of indigenous sovereignty in legal practices.

Contribution for Theoretical Area 1

(2) Indigenous sovereignty/Post-Westphalian concepts of sovereignty

Within the United States the argument that tribes are in some way equivalent to sovereign nations—nations within nations—has caused constant legal and political tension (Robertson 2007; Wilkinson 1987; Deloria 1998). Historically, Chief Justice John Marshall's trilogy of Indian cases in the 1820s and 30s held that tribes are not "foreign states" as envisaged under the American Constitution, but rather "domestic dependent nations" in "a state of pupilage". In short, a tribe's relation to the United States resembles that of a ward to his guardian (see *Johnson v M'Intosh* (1823)). More recently, in the *Santa Clara Pueblo* case of 1978, the Supreme Court defined tribes as "distinct, independent political communities, retaining their original natural rights... [but] no longer possessed of the full attributes of sovereignty... Congress has plenary authority to limit, modify or eliminate the powers of local self-government which the tribes otherwise possess". Interestingly, the concept of tribal sovereignty loses its power the more it engages with non-Indians. For instance in the Indian gaming case *San Manuel Indian Bingo & Casino* of 2007, the US Circuit Court of Appeals of Columbia held that "tribal sovereignty is not absolute autonomy, permitting a tribe to operate in a commercial capacity without legal constraint". Accordingly, tribal sovereignty is "weakest in off-reservation business transactions with non-members" (Wiessner 2008:1168). Ambiguities and inconsistencies with respect to the concept of tribal sovereignty continue to undermine Indian and non-Indian relations to this day (Wilkins 2008:244).

Common Knowledge for Theoretical Area 2 (indigenous sovereignty)

However, despite general confusion in federal and state Indian law over the meaning of native sovereignty, there do appear to be recognizable trends in judicial interpretation. Typically American courts interpret the concept of native sovereignty to accord with the institutional and economic interests of the state to the detriment of tribal interests. These interpretations stress that tribes do not hold inherent sovereign power and are only qualified to exercise any form of self-government because, by virtue of their status as "wards", that right has been delegated to them by the United States. As Thomas Biolsi notes, the court's idea of tribal sovereignty is, "limited, in fact, to the point that it does not make logical sense to many Indian people, is not really sovereignty at all from their point of view, and can only be understood as bespeaking a profoundly racist view of Indians on the part of Congress, the courts, and white people in general" (Biolsi 2005:243).

Indigenous perspectives on sovereignty often conflict with the classic Westphalian model of sovereignty upheld by the US Supreme Court and based upon power over peoples within a territory. Many native peoples typically interpret sovereignty as based in relations between people, place, and a sense of community. June McCue, director of First Nations Studies at University of British Columbia, writes "From an Indigenous perspective, sovereignty is not just human-centered and hierarchical; it is not solely born or sustained through brute force. Indigenous sovereignty must be birthed through a genuine effort to establish peace, respect,

Disruptor for Theoretical Area 2

and balance in this world. Indigenous sovereignty is interconnected with self-determination" (cited Wiessman 2008:1173). In a similar vein, Vine Deloria Jr. has argued that indigenous sovereignty "consists more of a continued cultural integrity than of political powers and to the degree a nation loses its sense of cultural identity, to that degree is suffers a loss of sovereignty" (Deloria 1996:123).

The proposed research will add to scholarly debates and literature on post-Westphalian concepts of sovereignty by exploring competing conceptualizations of the concept as it relates to and plays out in numerous interconnected legal arenas pertaining to native issues. While the proposed project engages explicitly with the concept of indigenous sovereignty it may have broader impact with respect to rethinking sovereignty and legal pluralism in the 21st century more generally.

Contribution for Theoretical Area 2

(3) Scholarship on Indian Gaming

The proposed research will also contribute to debates on Indian Gaming in the United States. Books on Indian gaming include Angela Mullis and David Kamper's *Indian Gaming: Who Wins?* (2000, UCLA American Indian Studies Center) and Dale Mason's *Indian Gaming: Tribal Sovereignty and American Politics* (2000, University of Oklahoma Press). Texts and casebooks specifically targeting legal practitioners and policy makers include William Eadington's *Indian Gaming and the Law* (1998, University of Nevada Press), Steven Light and Kathryn R. L. Rand *Indian Gaming*

Common Knowledge for Theoretical Area 3 (Indian Gaming)

and Tribal Sovereignty: The Casino Compromise (2005, University Press of Kansas), Kathryn R. L. Rand and Steven Light *Indian Gaming Law and Policy* (2006, Carolina Academic Press), and Steven Light and Kathryn R. L. Rand *Indian Gaming Law: Cases and Materials* (2007, Carolina Academic Press). These books point to a rich body of scholarship on Indian gaming.

However, none of these works engage with the issues specifically addressed in the proposed research; i.e. theoretical concerns with the revitalization of the concept of indigenous sovereignty and how this may relate to debates surrounding legal pluralism. Nor do these works take as their empirical foci Indian gaming's impact on multiple sites of law and governance and how these may relate to shifts in mainstream social attitudes toward Native Americans. Nor do these scholarly works engage with the future status of Native Americans in terms of connecting the relatively recent economic empowerment among a few tribes as a result of Indian gaming with new positions of political power in governmental bureaucracies and political activism.

Disruptor for Theoretical Area 3

INTELLECTUAL MERIT

First, this project will contribute to understanding and reassessing the place and presence of Native Americans in US society, law and governance in the 21st century, building upon critical race theories to frame the concept of indigenous rights as an issue of racial justice. This reassessment will pay particular attention to the impact of Indian gaming which has given some tribes the

Summary of Theoretical Contributions

capacity to participate in mainstream American life for the first time, and some Native Americans the opportunity to work in the highest levels of federal governmental agencies and administration.

Second, the proposed research will engage with different visions of sovereignty as they play out in local, state and federal law. It will explore and contrast how native peoples think about sovereignty with how mainstream American society, law and legal institutions interpret and deploy the concept. Building upon the work of scholars such as Frank Geyla and Carole Goldberg who have published a groundbreaking in-depth study of the historical struggle over sovereignty by the Tule River Tribe in California (who today own a very successful casino), this proposed research seeks to widen the conversation beyond specific tribes and explore the shifting place of native peoples in US society more generally.

Third, the proposed research will contribute to broader theoretical and empirical studies of sovereignty and nation-building in a post-Westphalian world. By focusing on the concept of indigenous sovereignty and its current revitalization and reframing in US local, state, and national law, the research examines the role tribes are playing as they "push back" and seek to reappropriate the concept in their own terms. The wider merit of the proposed research is its exploration of the dynamic constitutive relationship between non-western law and dominant western legal systems as they play out in the defining of sovereignty and nations. This exploration also

```
opens up conversations about legal
pluralism within national domestic
jurisdictions, which is often
unacknowledged and overlooked.
```

Summary

In this chapter we showed you how to contextualize your research contributions within the existing literature. Don't forget that the Theoretical Context and Significance section is about *you*; not about the authors and studies that you refer to in this section. As with the Introduction, this section is about "framing" your research within a highly strategic vision of your field that highlights your contributions. Using the common knowledge–disruptor pattern with a carefully edited set of theories and existing studies enables the reviewer to get on the same page and share your vision with ease.

In the next chapter, we teach you how to tackle the Methodology/Plan of Work section of the proposal, ensuring that it is convincing and tightly integrated with earlier proposal sections.

BOX 8.3   THEORETICAL ORIENTATION AND SIGNIFICANCE EXERCISE

1. Find two successful proposals (search online or ask peers and mentors).
2. Find two unsuccessful proposals (ask peers or mentors or perhaps look back at some of your own unsuccessful attempts).
3. Analyze the Theoretical Orientation and Significance sections of these proposals.
   a. Does the proposal use section headers?
   b. Is there a distinct Theoretical Orientation and Significance section?
   c. Does the section begin with metanarrative?
   d. Can you easily identify what areas of theory or scholarship are being reviewed?
   e. Can you easily identify how the proposed research will make contributions to the areas of theory or scholarship discussed?
   f. For each area of theory or scholarship reviewed:
      i. What is the common knowledge?
      ii. What is the disruptor?
      iii. Is the significance or contribution of the proposed research clear?
4. Compare the successful proposals against the unsuccessful proposals. What similarities and differences do you find?

9

WRITING THE METHODOLOGY/ PROCEDURES/PLAN OF WORK SECTION

The Methodology section is where many proposals go awry. Your Methods (or Procedures or Plan of Work) section cannot simply be a laundry list of what you plan to do with the grant or fellowship funding. In this section of the proposal you must convince the reviewers that you:

- Are experienced and adept at the practice of your research
- Are using the most suitable methods or procedures for your project
- Have the expertise to analyze and make sense of your data and materials in order to reach conclusions about your research questions

As a graduate student or junior faculty member, you may not have much independent research experience, if any at all. HSS graduate school coursework does not emphasize methods; most departments make do with one class that sums up methods for the entire discipline in one semester. As deftly described by Michael Watts (1999) in his essay on proposal writing: research "is a Darwinian learning-by-doing ordeal for which there is presumed to be no body of preparatory knowledge that can be passed on in advance; those that succeed return, and those that don't are never seen again."

Without sufficient training or experience in the "doing" of research, it can be difficult to write an authoritative Methodology section. This book, however, is not a guide on methods or research design, and we do not aim to tell you how you should go about actually doing your research. There are many wonderful methods books on the market that cover every possible procedure for the HSS disciplines. Between these and advice from your advisor and mentors, you will inevitably come up with a scheme by which you can carry out your research.

Even for those well versed in the art of research methods, writing about it can be perplexing. How does one technically describe "close reading," for example? How can you possibly make "participant observation" appear to be a systematic methodological procedure? In this chapter we provide advice on describing your methods in a way that is well organized and integrated with the other key sections, especially your theoretical significance and research questions. For every method that you plan to use, it must be:

• Explained in as much detail as space will allow
• Justified
• Linked specifically to the data, evidence, or materials necessary to answer your research questions or objectives

Methods Matrix Tool

A good way to think through the relationships and integration among the various proposal parts is to create a matrix. We have already covered this in Chapter 6 in relation to conceptualizing a strategic proposal, but it bears repeating here. The X and Y axes might be arranged in slightly different ways, depending on your project. In the following example (Table 9.1), we begin with the research questions and then connect the other components to each of these.

Using this kind of organizational tool can help you brainstorm and make decisions about precisely:

• What kinds of information you will collect
• Where it will come from
• How you will collect it
• How you will analyze or interpret it

Going through this exercise will also expose potential holes in your research questions and hypotheses. For instance, you might realize that certain types of data or materials that you had vaguely imagined don't actually exist, or your methods for getting access to materials are unfeasible. This process will take you from a hazy list

TABLE 9.1 Methods Matrix Tool

Research Question	Hypotheses/ Anticipated Outcomes	Data/ Evidence/ Materials	Theoretical Contribution	Method/ Procedure	Source	Analysis
Question 1						
Question 2						
Question 3						

of typical methods in your field (interviews, participant observation, and discourse analysis for example) to mapping out the nitty-gritty, such as:

- Who do I need to interview, and how many people?
- Should my sample be stratified in a certain way or is a random sample more appropriate to answer my research question?
- How will I get those people to talk to me?
- What kinds of things am I looking for when I observe the factory workers?
- How do I collect or record this information?
- Are the newspaper articles online, or will I have to visit the archives in a foreign country?

The Methods section in your proposal can be organized in several different ways. For example, some organize it around each research question or hypothesis. Some organize it around the methods or procedures themselves. There is no one right answer, and you need to follow the logic of your particular project. Whichever way you decide to go, you should include the following information:

- A thorough description of the method or procedure and how you will apply it.
- If the method is uncommon, it can be useful to cite particularly important studies that have used it. However, citing the method alone is not enough information for the reviewer. You must also describe what you will do and why it is ideal for your research.
- The specific types of data, information, or materials the method will produce or extract.
- How the collected information constitutes evidence for your research questions or hypotheses.
- How the data or materials, once collected, will be analyzed.

Differences and Similarities in Humanities and Social Science Methods

Our approach to proposal writing is fundamentally the same for both humanities and social sciences in terms of overall conceptual development and writing strategies. However, in reference to the Methodology/Plan of Work section of the proposal, there is a wide spectrum of humanities and social science approaches that deserves special attention here. The difference in approaches has been characterized, for example, as empirical (social sciences) vs. interpretive (humanities) modes of analysis. Many social scientists and humanists employ a variety of methods that fall along this continuum, sometimes using a combination of social science and humanities methods in one research project. We have also seen a recent blurring of the lines between the two. For example, the advent of the digital humanities marks a turn toward the use of quantitative methods with humanities materials.

As we emphasized in Chapter 3, knowing the culture and funding portfolio of your target funding agency is critical. For example, the National Endowment for the Humanities (NEH) will not fund an economics research project, of course, but they also are unlikely to fund a humanities project that includes a significant share of qualitative social science methods. The emphasis at NEH is *interpretive humanities* research. Ergo, if you are an interdisciplinary researcher who uses both social science and humanities methods in your research and you are applying for funding from the NEH, you should frame your proposal around the interpretive analysis. Save the social science analysis for another funding agency. Likewise, the way you describe a particular method could vary depending on the agency to which you are applying. For instance, "close reading" and "computational text analysis" are two sides of the same coin. It is your job to find out how your target agency views these methods and which they are more likely to fund. Insights can be gleaned from studying abstracts of what your target agency has already funded.

Regardless of the methods that you employ, it is important to remember that they should be described rigorously and in detail.

Capturing the Elusive Method

What do close reading, participant observation, and discourse analysis have in common? They are all examples of humanistic and qualitative research methods that are difficult to describe, particularly as there is not always a step-by-step procedure for performing these types of methods. Likewise, qualitative and interpretive analyses are not necessarily methodical, or reducible to patterns or numbers, in the ways that empirical and quantitative research is. Even when there is a clear standard for the method in academe, we find that certain types of methods (interviews, for example) are troublesome for some HSS researchers to write about. A related problem is that conceptions and understandings of these methods are implicit or tacit knowledge in HSS disciplines. As a result, we see time and again that researchers give very short shrift to explaining details about these methods in their proposals, assuming that the reviewers will intuitively know what they are talking about. However, even if the reviewer "knows what you are talking about," they also want to be convinced that *you* know what you are talking about. As we emphasize throughout this book, it is imperative to gauge the level of detail and description that you need to provide by studying sample successful proposals as templates for formatting and scope and thoroughly investigating how interdisciplinary (or disciplinary) your review panel might be. Following are a few examples of methods that seem particularly problematic in HSS proposals.

Fieldwork

Whether you are going to a foreign country for a year of ethnographic research or going to the archives to study ancient documents, you need to convince reviewers about why and where you are going. To do this, be specific. Name the precise location, such as the village where you will live and interview people, or the precise archive and its contents that you will examine. Depending on your research and your intended destination, it may also make sense to explain *when* you are going. Will the season or local labor patterns affect your ability to interview informants? A reviewer will not be convinced if you plan to interview farmers during the harvest season, for example. Also, indicate that you have access to your subjects or materials. If you are going to be interviewing people or working with organizations, explain that you have made prior contacts and arrangements to meet people in this community. Also indicate that you speak/read the necessary foreign language or have plans to hire a translator.

Another problem we often see is related to "convenience" field sites. Many people default to a location in which to do their research simply because it is where they live or it is nearby. Instead, you should choose your research location because it is ideal in specific reference to your theoretical contribution and research questions. This becomes more important with comparative sites. You will need to make a clear case for why the two or more sites provide similarities and differences that have bearing on your research questions. Two sites aren't necessarily better than one unless there is a significant way in which the comparison of the two will have implications for your contribution to the literature.

Above all, don't "hope" for anything related to your fieldwork, and don't let on to the possibility that you won't be able to make certain arrangements or decisions until you get to your research location. Reviewers and program officers want to be convinced that you have a rock-solid plan that is absolutely ready to go.

Talking to People

If you are conducting interviews, surveys, focus groups, or oral histories, reviewers want to know a lot about your informants and procedures. You cannot state nebulously that you will "interview ten key informants," or "100 subjects," and then move on. Provide details about:

- Whom you will interview and why you chose them.
- How many people and why that number is sufficient or ideal.
- The sample: Is it random, purposive, snowball, or convenience, for example, and why is it the appropriate or best sample of people to talk to?
- Stratification of the sample—what types of people (gender, ethnicity, age, rank, etc.), and why is difference or sameness significant to the analysis?
- How will you get access to the people you want to talk to? How will you reward or incentivize them?
- Information about the types of questions you will ask and why. What information from each category of questions will provide evidence for your research questions?
- Provide a clear explanation of the data collection mechanics, such as will you take notes or tape record and transcribe interviews? Will the survey be online? Are there language and translation issues that you need to discuss?

- The analysis is also important to describe. Once you have your pile of transcribed interviews, then what? How will you study these to make sense of them? Will you use software (statistical or qualitative analysis tools such as NVivo or Dedoose?).
- The instruments. It is increasingly common to see actual interview and survey instruments attached as appendices to proposals. Find out from the program officer if this would be a strategic addition to your proposal.
- IRB approval. As with the instruments, IRB approval is increasingly necessary for final grant approval from federal agencies. Alluding to any IRB issues and your progress toward having an approved protocol should be mentioned in your Methods section if appropriate.

Participant Observation

Participant observation is frequently used as a key method in ethnographic field research. Some refer to it as "serious hanging out." In many social science and humanities proposals, we see this method mentioned with little explanation for exactly what the researcher intends to do. The challenge in describing this method in a rigorous research proposal is to be clear about:

- The setting in which you are using this method and why it is an ideal locale in which to collect the information necessary for your research
- The ways that you are participating and how your participation intersects with the information that you are collecting
- What you will be looking for in your observations (i.e., what counts as data), such as specific relationships, actions, language, etc.
- How you will record and analyze your observations

Close Reading

To reviewers who are not familiar with this method, a proposal describing close reading can seem a lot like this: "Please give me a lot of money so that I can buy a stack of books, go into my office, and read them for a year." If you are applying for a grant from the National Endowment for the Humanities, for example, you can feel confident that your reviewers will have a better understanding of close reading than this. But if you know that your review panel will be interdisciplinary, you will need to spend some time describing how close reading results in the evidence or information that is necessary for your research. In either case, you must be clear about why you have chosen the specific books or other materials; what language, ideas, or themes you are paying attention to throughout your reading; and how you will record, analyze, and/or interpret these in relationship to your research questions and your contributions to your field.

Archival Materials

Archival research lends itself to another oft-repeated Methods section faux pas. Archival research is frequently described in proposals as a "visit" to the archives. Although you may be a *visiting* fellow at an archive, your work in the archives should be explained in more detail than the word "visit" conjures. Do not say you will do research in an archive on a hunch about what documents might lie therein. As an expert in your field, reviewers will expect you to know the contents of the relevant archives and how the materials provide information or evidence for your research. If you are not sure, contact the archive staff or inquire with others who have used your target archives. Provide a detailed explanation in your Methods section about the materials you will study, such as types of materials, the sources of the materials, the period covered, the volume of materials, and so forth. What specifically from these materials are you looking for, and how does this information answer your research questions?

Quantitative Analysis

For those of you who do quantitative research in the social sciences and humanities, it is crucial to understand that you use a specific form of jargon, namely math equations and statistical analyses. If your proposal goes to an interdisciplinary review panel, you can be sure that many of the reviewers will not be able to understand it. We have served on countless review panels where a "bilingual" reviewer in the group serves as a translator for the panel, explaining what the quantitative proposal means and why it is important. You don't want this to be your proposal! You should not rely on one member of a review panel to be able to explain it to a larger group of reviewers.

To avoid this scenario, you need to strategically write the proposal for two audiences. Although you must show your methodological expertise in mathematical detail, it is equally important to explain this in plain English to the reviewers who do qualitative research. Some of the reviewers will not be familiar with the assumptions that go into quantitative analyses, let alone the analytical mechanics, so you must describe the bigger picture of how your analysis answers the broader questions that you ask in your research. Use metanarrative to foreground the Methods section for the qualitative audience, and do not presume that your math equations will speak for themselves.

Risk, Uncertainty, and Ethics

Like war, no research campaign goes exactly as planned. You will certainly experience a few breakdowns in the supply chain (no key informants will let you interview them during the entire month of Ramadan), a few bombs may blow up in your face (a flood swamps your archive during an unexpected storm), and some of your soldiers might go AWOL (after a grueling six months of research in the Amazon, you are medivac-ed to Quito for dengue fever and never make it back to the field). You do not have to explicate every potential skirmish, setback, and contingency plan in your proposal. As we point out in Chapter 6, you need to tell a convincing story and stick to it, even if you are fudging some of the minor details.

For major details, however, the Methods section is a good place to discuss the riskier and exploratory aspects of your research that are there by design. Do not leave any "white elephants" in the proposal by glossing over obvious risks that the reviewers and program officer will recognize. If there is civil unrest in the country of your intended field site, for example, you should explain that you have made the necessary arrangements and appropriate contacts to safely work there. If the documents you intend to study are notoriously difficult to access, make a case for how you have taken the proper steps to ensure that you will be able to read them. If the method that you are using is untested, explain the alternative plans that you have in place to salvage the research. Some agencies may ask you to discuss your human or animal subjects compliance plans in your proposal. Even if not asked, you should acknowledge the compliance issues in your proposal if you are working with a particularly sensitive group (children, for example). Particularly in cases where you are studying human or animal subjects, it is crucial to convey your competent knowledge of the legal and ethical approaches to working with these subjects.

Methods/Procedures Section Examples

In the following two examples we illustrate effective formats for writing the Methods section. These excerpts emphasize that details are important and that you cannot assume the reviewers will "know what I mean" when you hazily reference your plan to do "oral history" or "focus groups," for example.

BOX 9.1 PROPOSAL EXCERPT: METHODS/PROCEDURES SECTION FROM A PROPOSAL TO THE NATIONAL SCIENCE FOUNDATION

Title: Doing Due Diligence: Forms of Moral Judgment in the Regulation of International Finance

Author: William Maurer, PhD, Anthropology

This proposal was funded by a grant from the National Science Foundation (NSF) Law and Social Sciences program. The Methods section is an excellent example of how to describe qualitative methods in a rigorous way. It also includes a Data Analysis section, which many HSS proposal writers tend to leave out of proposals. Notice that the section starts with a paragraph of metanarrative, and the entire section is punctuated by subheaders to keep the reviewer on track. The page limits for an NSF proposal (fifteen pages) allow for this extensive treatment of the methods.

Methodology

The proposed research relies on archival and ethnographic methods. Ethnographic fieldwork will be conducted in the British Virgin Islands for a total of 6 months divided into two three-month periods. Archival research will take place in the British Virgin Islands and in Irvine, California, using the facilities of the University of California library system. Many archival sources are also publicly available online through the websites of the IOs and NGOs involved in soft law attempts to curtail harmful tax practices.

1) Archival research, British Virgin Islands

   The PI will collect and build a database of archival material relating to the following:

   a) BVI legislation and statutory orders relating to offshore financial services, pre- and post-1998 (the date of the first OECD report on harmful tax practices). In addition to the actual laws and statutory instruments, an archive will be built from Legislative Council and Executive Council minutes which are publicly available (but not catalogued) in the archives of the Government of the British Virgin Islands. The PI has experience working with these archives, having compiled the first index to Legislative and Executive Council documents for the British Virgin Islands Public Library in 1992-93. The Legislative and Executive Councils are the governing bodies of the British Virgin Islands; the Legislative Council is elected by the people of the territory; the Executive Council is appointed by the Governor (who in turn is appointed by the Crown). In previous research, the PI found Legislative Council documents in particular to illuminate British Virgin Islander conceptions of law, justice and virtue as well as to provide important behind-the-scenes accounts of the drafting and debate over legislative and administrative change in the territory (see Maurer 1997). The PI will also collect archival material from the newly-established Financial Services Commission, including promotional material and governing documents.

   b) Public commentary on the OECD and other initiatives against harmful tax practices. The two main newspapers, the *Island Sun* and the *BVI Beacon*, are expected to have published editorials and letters to the editor about the "naming and shaming" initiative against tax havens in addition to journalistic accounts.

   c) Pedagogical and training material. The H. Lavity Stoutt Community College provides postsecondary education for British Virgin Islanders seeking employment in the financial services sector. The PI will collect syllabi, course materials, reading lists, as well as training manuals used in classes and in seminars, and whatever material may be archived from prior conferences on due diligence (there have been three such conferences so far). Pedagogical and training material provided by multinational consultancy firms, registered agents, and law offices in the BVI, will also be collected.

d) Redacted letters of reference and curricula vitae filed by potential financial services clients for due diligence purposes. The PI will build an archive of redacted due diligence materials from two corporate service companies operating in the BVI: one with a majority British Virgin Islander staff, and one with a majority expatriate staff. The two companies will be selected based on comparability in terms of size (number of employees, number of clients) and duration of operation in the territory. Contact will be established through the PI's existing relationships in the British Virgin Islands as well as through the H. Lavity Stoutt Community College and the Financial Services Commission.

2) Archival research, United States

The PI will build an archive of relevant documents relating to the transnational advocacy network working on tax competition and harmful preferential tax regimes. This will include all reports and public statements issued by the OECD, FATF, Financial Stability Forum, Basel Committee on Banking Supervision, and other IOs as well as Oxfam, Christian Aid and other NGOs that have issued policy statements on tax competition. The PI will also build an archive of material produced by scholar-activists working on tax competition, such as the network of scholars affiliated with the Tax Justice Network and the Association for Accountancy and Business Affairs, which has sponsored academic conferences on reducing tax competition and has been involved in drafting statements of principles for NGOs such as Oxfam.

3) Participant observation, British Virgin Islands

Due to the nature of the topic of this research, it cannot be expected that people will always respond to questions in formal interviews in a manner commensurate with their actual beliefs, practices and taken for granted assumptions. Therefore, participant observation is absolutely vital to the success of the proposed research. It is difficult to specify in advance the kinds of activities participant observation might end up entailing. Nevertheless, the following list comprises the most important venues for this research activity.

The PI will participate in the following activities and institutional settings:

a) H. Lavity Stoutt Community College: The PI will attend training sessions, seminars and symposia on due diligence. The PI has had a research affiliation with this institution in the past.

b) Financial Services Commission: The PI will regularly visit the offices of the FSC and build rapport with its staff.

c) Two corporate services companies. The PI will work as an unpaid volunteer doing due diligence in two corporate services companies, one with a predominantly BV Islander staff, and one with a predominantly expatriate staff.

d) Churches and rum shops. In order to determine whether due diligence is spilling over into other domains of life in the BVI, the PI will regularly attend church services and corner rum shops, two institutions central to BV Islander social life and around which the discourse on respectability and reputation is organized.

Informal interviews will occur continuously during the work of participant observation, particularly with the following types of people, among others: teachers at the HLSCC who teach due diligence, staff of the FSC, staff of corporate service companies, lawyers, and priests and pastors.

Data analysis

1) Archival material collected in the British Virgin Islands.

With the exception of redacted due diligence documents, the archival material collected in the BVI will be analyzed for trends in reporting, argument, and metaphor in the discussion of due diligence, the OECD and other global initiatives, and transformations in the offshore financial services sector since 1998. Redacted due diligence material will be subjected to a content analysis using methods similar to those developed for the analysis of letters of recommendation to detect gender bias (see Trix and Psenka 2003 on content analysis of letters of recommendation for academic employment). Then, they will be crosstabulated with participant observation and interview data from the two corporate services firms in order to determine what elements of letters of recommendation impact which kinds of ethical judgments. Graduate student research assistants will be trained to assist in the analysis of this data.

2) Archival material collected in the United States.

In addition to documenting the history of the effort to reduce harmful tax practices, the PI will analyze these documents in terms of historical shifts in the use of specific terms or metaphors (for example, the emergence of the term "harm" to describe tax competition rather than "crime") and correlate these to the rise of specific IO or NGO initiatives. Does a common language emerge over time? What new terms get introduced once the language seems relatively settled? Where do these new terms originate? If local discourses of ethics are inflecting the global epistemic community, then terms, metaphors, anecdotes, and turns of phrase with Caribbean provenience may begin to appear in these "international" documents. Graduate student research assistants will be trained to assist in the analysis of this data.

3 and 4) Participant observation and Interviews, British Virgin Islands.

In conducting participant observation, the PI will be particularly attentive to the moral and evaluative discourses brought to bear on the work of due diligence, the reputation/respectability dichotomy, and any apparent influences of the one on the other or vice versa. The PI will also be attentive to instances where due diligence—the term, the concepts used, signal features of the public debate about it, etc.—crops up in other domains, such as sermons, calypso songs or other performances, slang, rum shop talk, and so forth.

The PI will learn the "official" methods of conducting due diligence in the BVI. This will be compared with other practitioner texts and trainings, as well as the practice on the ground in the two corporate services companies. At the two companies, the PI will do due diligence with the other staff, and learn the formal and informal methods by which those doing due diligence make judgment calls on the documents that come before them. Are there any phrases or arguments in letters of recommendation that clinch a case, one way or another? Is there a set of discourses or specific practices regarding the "file" versus the "client" (the distancing move of claiming that one "judges the file, not the client," and that any shortcomings can be remedied by requests for additional information to be added to the file, for example)? What kind of knowledge do people think they are gaining when they enact Know Your Customer procedures? How do they evaluate their potential customers, as well as this knowledge?

In conducting participation observation with financial services employees, the PI will also attempt to discern the formal elements of the kinds of moral evaluation being used to assess a potential client. Is the mode of ethical evaluation based on rules and obligations (deontology); on cost benefit or means-ends calculations (utilitarian); on notions of human flourishing (virtue ethics; i.e., "just by doing this work of due diligence, no matter the outcome for a particular case, we are doing good")? Finally, the PI will compare the techniques and moral arguments of BV Islanders and expatriates to see whether other normative universes or epistemic or cognitive orientations come in to play in the making of judgments.

BOX 9.2   PROPOSAL EXCERPT: METHODS/PROCEDURES SECTION FROM A PROPOSAL TO THE AMERICAN COUNCIL OF LEARNED SOCIETIES RYSKAMP FELLOWSHIP

Title: Akosombo Stories: The Volta River Project, Modernity, and Nationhood in Ghana

Author: Stephan Miescher, PhD, History

This section comes from a proposal funded by the American Council for Learned Societies (ACLS) within a much shorter format (six-page limit, including bibliography). It provides a detailed account of the work plan, specific information about the archives and interviews, and how the proposed work fits in to the investigator's overall research and publication schedule. Note that the proposal author also reassures reviewers about his level of access to the materials and subjects, explaining his facility with the language, his established networks of scholars, his prior experience in the archives, and contacts among potential interview participants.

Sources and Work Schedule

This project grows out of my first book, *Making Men in Ghana* (2005), which explores how a group of Kwawu men dealt with modernity and new ideas of masculinity. I developed a research methodology combining archival work with extensive oral history research, and creating conversations between the two. Kwawu is an Akan area whose northern part was affected by Lake Volta's flooding. I am familiar with Ghana's major archives and have built a network of contacts with Ghanaian scholars. I have also acquired a knowledge of Twi, which facilitates interviewing.

I have already gathered material for this project including government records, VRA reports, and unpublished social science papers. I examined microfilms of Ghanaian newspapers available in the U.S. During the summer of 2005, I located the VRA archive in Tema and established contacts with the ATL management, which assured me access to its archive. I identified documents about the Volta River Project in Ghana's National Archives in Accra and Koforidua. Last December I conducted research at Rhodes House, Oxford and the Public Record Office, London. In July 2006 I returned to Ghana and continued my archival work. In 2005, I also did preliminary oral research in Ghana. In interviews with market women I learned how Akosombo has become a generic name for wax prints produced in Ghana, associated with non-elite status. I visited the resettlement town of Amate in the Afram Plains, where I recorded people's recollections about a time of abundance prior to

Lake Volta. They expressed a sense of loss, commenting on unfulfilled government promises. Now they are facing hardships due to climate change. In 2006, I visited Akosombo Township to establish contacts, and continued my interviews in Amate.

I would begin an ACLS fellowship in September 2007. By then I will have drafted chapter one and part of chapter two. During a ten-month stay in Ghana, I will complete archival research in the National Archives in Accra, Koforidua, Ho, and Tamale and in the VRA archive, and consult ATL company records in Accra. In the Akosombo township I plan to conduct thirty interviews with current and former VRA employees and their families, some of whom I have identified during my visit last summer. I will complete my interviews in resettlement towns of the Afram Plains and talk with former settlers who left the once fertile plains. Oral research will complement archival documents on electrification: one set of interviews will be conducted in the Accra urban area, another in a small rural town only recently connected to the grid. I will continue my conversations with ATL representatives, as well as market women and their customers, to learn more about the consumption of Ghanaian cloth. I will interview former Akosombo Dam tour guides and artists, such as highlife singer Obibini Takyi, who feature Akosombo in their work. In Ghana I will continue writing to reflect on my research. July and August 2008 will be spent in Santa Barbara, evaluating documents and interviews, and writing. An ACLS fellowship would provide crucial support to complete the research for this project.

Summary

In this chapter, we have given you guidelines for communicating the "what" and "how" of your research project in the most compelling way. Remember that details are important in the Methodology/Plan of Work section. Reviewers and program officers want to be convinced that if they approve your proposal, you will hit the ground running with a thorough plan of action, including contingencies for potential setbacks. Even qualitative and interpretive methods should be explained in detail and described methodically. It is also crucial that the methods are closely tied to the prior proposal parts, with a plan of work that collects and analyzes information that speaks directly to answering your research questions and making your stated contributions to the literature.

By now, the most important sections of your proposal are written. You have presented a coherent and convincing plan focused around compelling research questions that are grounded in, and contribute to, the relevant literature on your topic. Next we get to the main point of all this writing: asking for the money! In the next chapter we teach you how to build your budget and how to explain it to reviewers.

BOX 9.3 METHODS/PROCEDURES EXERCISE

1. Find two successful proposals (search online or ask peers and mentors).
2. Find two unsuccessful proposals (ask peers or mentors or perhaps look back at some of your own unsuccessful attempts).
3. Analyze the Methodology/Plan of Work sections of these proposals.
    a. Does the proposal use section headers?
    b. Is there a distinct Methodology/Plan of Work section?
    c. Does the section begin with metanarrative?
    d. Can you easily identify what methods are being employed?
    e. Are the methods linked to the research questions and evidence needed to answer them?
    f. How much detail is provided for each method?
    g. How does the proposal describe the data analysis?
    h. Is there a timeline that describes a reasonable sequence of work and activities?
4. Compare the successful proposals against the unsuccessful proposals. What similarities and differences do you find?

10

WRITING THE BUDGET AND BUDGET JUSTIFICATION

The budget to a large extent determines the scope of your work. Before you begin to write your proposal, you will need to think about the budget and how it relates to your research plan. Indeed, the budget oftentimes dictates the scope of your research plan and the types of methods that you can undertake in your research. Everything in the budget must be justified by the work you propose to do, and vice versa. Get started on your budget as soon as you begin to write your proposal. It is a compelling piece of your story and another way to convey that you are prepared to hit the ground running with your project once funded. You don't want it to detract from your otherwise excellent proposal.

Although it is impossible to estimate every cost down to the penny, you should be as accurate as possible in your budget. In the typical grant cycle, you will write your budget six months to a year before you start to spend the money. A lot can change in twelve months. For example, the price of gas, and thus the cost of airfare or other transportation, can rise or fall dramatically. Inflation in a foreign country can send food and lodging costs in your field site skyrocketing. You might get an unexpected accelerated promotion and your summer salary costs will increase by 10%. Regardless, your proposal budget should be the best possible estimate of your actual costs. Once the award is in, budget adjustments can be made with guidance from your institution's Sponsored Projects Office and the agency program officer.

The budget is one area of your proposal where you should work closely with your campus Office of Sponsored Projects and/or your Research Development Office. There are many figures that you will not necessarily have access to, such as:

- Graduate student researcher salaries
- Fringe benefit rates
- Indirect cost rates

It is possible that your campus can furnish you with a budget template to work with or that there is a dedicated grant budget specialist on your campus who can create a budget for you.

Fellowships

Before we get into the nitty-gritty on itemized budgets, it is important to note here that some funding opportunities do not require a budget at all. These are usually fellowships that come with a one-size-fits-all sum. Take the NEH fellowships, for example. Their Fellowship Guidelines indicate that:

> Fellowships cover periods lasting from six to twelve months at a stipend of $4,200 per month. The maximum stipend is $50,400 for a twelve-month period. Applicants should request award periods that suit their schedules and the needs of their projects . . . The award period must be **full-time** and **continuous**. Teaching and administrative assignments or other major activities may not be undertaken during the fellowship period [original emphasis].

The NEH application does not require an itemized budget or justification. They do not want to know precisely how you will spend the $4,200 per month beyond "full-time and continuous" work.

For these kinds of funding opportunities, it is important to discuss your options with various people at your institution, such as your department chair, your dean, and/or your Sponsored Projects Office. It may also be worthwhile to consult with your tax accountant. When talking to these people, you should consider the following questions:

- Will this fellowship cover my normal salary? If not, how will I make ends meet?
- Who will teach my courses while I am on this fellowship?
- Who will take over my administrative responsibilities while I am on this fellowship?
- Can I combine multiple awards, fellowships, and/or grants with this fellowship?
- How does my sabbatical fit in with this award?
- Can I transfer the fellowship funds to my institution and then continue to receive my regular salary, benefits, and service credits?
- Can I convert this fellowship to summer salary, course buyout, or release time?
- If I accept this fellowship, will it constitute personal taxable income?

Budgets and Proposal Strategy

In helping faculty and students develop research proposals, we are frequently asked if the budget can make or break a proposal. For example:

> "Should I lowball my budget and request only a fraction of the amount that my competitors request, to give me a better chance of winning the grant?"

"If the funding limit is $100,000, will reviewers be suspicious that my budget coincidentally adds up to $99,999.99?"

"If I get the grant, I know the agency is automatically going to knock off 10% of the budget. So shouldn't I 'pad' the budget by 10%?"

The answer to all of these questions is yes and no. It depends on individual reviewers, the program officer, and the funding agency. In some competitions you indeed may have a higher chance of winning a grant if your budget is considerably smaller than all of the others. Program officers weigh a variety of criteria to achieve "portfolio balance" when choosing the final awards from a pool of meritorious proposals. In certain cases, funding two small awards over one big award may be advantageous to the agency. We have explicitly heard from some program officers that they are looking for "bang for the buck." With other agencies, the size of the budget isn't considered a factor in determining who receives an award.

In any case, budgets are typically scrutinized by program officers, if not reviewers, and they should be detailed and reasonable. Your budget should convey that you will have sufficient resources to carry out the proposed research. It is never a good idea to sell yourself short in your budget. You do not want to end up, for example, living in a youth hostel in your field site, begging students to volunteer their time on your project, or cutting out substantive components of your methodology because you didn't ask for enough money to complete the work properly.

Some agencies provide budget and project duration limits in their proposal guidelines, and others don't. In the case of the agencies that don't provide limits, understand that this does *not* mean that the sky is the limit. For these opportunities, it is important to study the agency website to gauge what they have funded in the past. Many agencies post titles, abstracts, dates, and funding amounts of their prior awards. What is the average amount they have awarded? What is the average duration of their grants? Using this information as a guide, you should design your project to be within the norms for your target agency. If the research project you have in mind falls outside of the typical grants that they are funding, either in duration or dollar amount, this is a good time to contact the program officer. They will let you know if your proposal idea has a chance of funding.

Budget Categories

We do not attempt to cover every detail about budgets in this book, and we encourage you to work with your appropriate campus experts in developing your budget. What you can and can't buy with research funds may be governed by multiple organizations, including the federal government, the funding agency, and/or your institution. As with all parts of a proposal, it is extremely useful to get copies of successful examples that were funded by your target agency. Seeing how your colleagues have formulated their budgets for similar research will give you a good idea of what is necessary, reasonable, and allowable.

In general, notwithstanding agency guidelines, a research budget typically consists of the following categories:

- Personnel
- Travel
- Equipment and supplies
- Other costs
- Indirect costs

Many funding agencies will provide you with a budget template or list of allowable categories as part of their RFP. By all means, follow their guidelines. If they say they won't fund computers or salary, for example, then do not put these items in your budget. Attempting to skirt their rules will only irritate reviewers and program officers, and may contribute to an unfavorable review of your proposal. However, if you are funding a project with multiple grants, it might make sense to submit your full budget to each agency, explaining how each agency is being asked to cover various parts of the budget.

Even for a simple budget, we suggest using a spreadsheet. This will ensure that the math is accurate. Submitting a proposal in which the budget does not add up correctly is a sign of a hastily written, last minute effort, and does not engender confidence in your work. If the proposal guidelines ask you to include the budget in the proposal narrative, use a table format. Do not lay out your budget in paragraph form.

The following sections provide key budget tips that come up most frequently in our consultations with faculty and students.

Personnel

The agency will usually provide guidelines on whether they will pay for salary, whether for you or a student, and how much they will pay for and when. Although salary support is often available through fellowships, many HSS grants will not fund salary. Instead, the funding is focused on the research itself. This can be frustrating for HSS faculty because one of our biggest needs in conducting research is the time off from teaching and other campus duties to devote to our research project.

Even for agencies that fund a salary, note that there can be unwritten conventions that dictate how much is typically requested or granted. For example, the National Science Foundation Proposal and Award Policies and Procedures Guide (PAPPG) states that NSF will pay for a maximum of two months of investigator salary in any one year of a grant. However, it is increasingly rare that investigators request or receive two months of summer salary, particularly from the cash-strapped Directorate for Social, Behavioral and Economic Sciences (SBE) programs. For example, in 2015, the average months of paid summer salary on an NSF SBE grant was 1.1 months (Report to the National Science Board on the National Science Foundation's Merit Review Process Fiscal Year 2015, p. 84). Check with program officers and your colleagues to find out what the conventions are for a given agency or at your institution.

On the other hand, HSS grants often provide funding for student assistance, albeit at a limited level. It is increasingly rare for an HSS grant to pay for the entire salary for a graduate student researcher or assistant, with full tuition and benefits, throughout the course of your project. More often, grants will cover an hourly wage for student assistance with discrete parts of your research.

As mentioned earlier, engage in a conversation with your chair, dean, and other relevant people on your campus when determining how grants salary intersects with your regular university income and responsibilities and the funding available for your students.

Travel

There are many reasons why you might need to travel for your research. Consider the research itself—traveling to a field site or archive, for example—as well as meeting with collaborators, or flying to conferences to present the results of your research. When budgeting for travel, do not ballpark anything. The Internet is awash with search engines that can help you find, reserve, and/or buy almost everything that you will need for your research. To estimate the costs of travel in your budget, use an Internet search engine and get real-time costs, including taxes.

For example, you need to conduct archival research in the State Archive of the Russian Federation for your historical study of Tsarist-era culinary trends and regional environmental management. For your flight to Moscow, search an online travel booking site, and choose one of the more reasonable prices that comes up in your search. Should you take the cheapest flight that has five layovers on an air carrier with the worst safety record? Not necessarily, although if you are working with a small grant or fellowship, then this may be one way to stretch the budget.

On the other hand, do not opt for first class, and do not assume that the grant will pay for premium seats with extra leg room. With federal funding, there is often the requirement that you fly on U.S. carriers. Airfare prices differ radically depending on the season, so do a search for the actual dates (or at least in the same month) that you anticipate traveling. Make sure that you budget for baggage fees and ground transportation to and from the airport.

As for room and board in Moscow, use the same Internet search process to estimate accommodations and food costs. For longer stays, look into the possibility of visiting scholar housing at local colleges and universities, or estimate the price of a rented apartment. For shorter stays, find a reasonable hotel in the most convenient location for your research.

In general, do not use the U.S. government "per diem" rate guidelines to estimate your travel budget. For domestic travel, the per diem rates are determined by the General Services Administration, and for foreign travel, by the Department of State. These rates are searchable on the Internet and should be considered the maximum prices that a federal government employee would pay on business travel. For example, the current per diem rates for Moscow are $351 per day for lodging and $112 per day for meals and incidentals. These rates far exceed what a graduate student or faculty member would typically pay on a research trip and will likely be considered extravagant by proposal reviewers and program officers.

Equipment and Supplies

For federal grants, equipment is only referred to as "equipment" if it costs at least $5,000. But as humanists and social scientists, many of you may be scratching your head and wondering, "What piece of research equipment could I possibly buy that would cost over $5,000?" Given that our types of research do not typically require major instrumentation or large pieces of equipment, it is safe to say that this category will not apply to your research very often. Supplies, however, might include a wide variety of items needed for your research, such as:

- Laptop computer
- Portable scanner
- Voice recorder
- Camera
- Books
- Paper for printing interview instruments
- Notebooks and pencils for taking field notes
- Software for image editing or data analysis

Other Costs

Beyond supplies and materials, there are several other categories of costs that you should take into consideration when building your budget. These include:

- Subcontracts for consultants or translation and transcription services
- Photocopying charges in the archive
- International telephone and fax tolls
- Human subjects payments or incentives for the people you interview
- Postage
- Publication fees

As with travel, for each item listed here, be specific. If you are buying equipment such as a camera, computer, or scanner, write out the exact make and model. Name the software that you will use. Include the total costs with taxes and shipping in your budget. And provide names of subcontractors, if available.

Indirect Costs

When preparing a budget for a federal agency, costs fall under two general categories: direct and indirect costs. According to the federal Office of Management and Budget Uniform Administrative Requirements, Cost Principles, and Audit

Requirements for Federal Awards (commonly called the Uniform Guidance), direct costs are:

> those costs that can be identified specifically with a particular final cost objective, such as a Federal award, or other internally or externally funded activity, or that can be directly assigned to such activities relatively easily with a high degree of accuracy.
>
> *(Section § 200.413)*

Direct costs include the previously mentioned variety of supplies, materials, and services that you will need to conduct your research. This list will vary based on your particular project and methodology.

Indirect costs (also known as facilities and administrative costs—"F&A") are funds that you *sometimes* need to include in your grant budget. These funds are not for your research project per se, but instead go directly to your institution for "overhead," which includes things like the operation and maintenance of campus facilities and equipment and general administrative support.

In contrast to the definition of direct costs, indirect costs are "those [costs] that are incurred for common or joint objectives and therefore cannot be identified readily and specifically with a particular sponsored project, an instructional activity, or any other institutional activity" (OMB Uniform Guidance Appendix III to Part 200). Every university and college has an individually negotiated overhead rate with the federal government, and the rate is renegotiated from time to time. The rates range from about 20% to 70%.

This is another area in proposal development where it is important to work with the relevant Office of Research or Sponsored Projects personnel on your campus, who can help you navigate this terrain. Overhead rates are not applied to every budget category in your budget. Each institution may have variable rates depending on the grant activity (research vs. training, for example), and where it takes place (on campus or off campus). Many funding agencies and foundations put a cap on what overhead rate they will pay, and most colleges and universities comply with these caps. Certain types of projects, such as outreach or educational programming, may qualify you for an indirect cost waiver from your institution.

Cost-Share or Matching Funds

Cost-share and matching funds refer to cash and in-kind support for your project beyond what you request from a funding agency. This might include a cash contribution from your Office of Research or dean, or in-kind support such as a portion of your salary or departmental administrative support that can be counted toward the work on a grant project. This support typically comes from your university, but it could also come from other grants or fellowships for the same project. Investigators often think that including cost-share will improve the competitive advantage of their proposal. This is not usually the case, and unless it is required by the agency (Mandatory Cost Share), it should not be included in your budget.

However, a few agencies (or programs within agencies) expect to see match or cost-share in your budget, even though they don't explicitly require it in their proposal guidelines (Voluntary Cost Share). If you have any doubts about this spoken or unspoken policy for a given agency, contact the program officer and seek advice from researchers who have been previously funded by the agency.

The Budget Justification

Beyond the numbers, you are usually required to include a budget justification along with your budget. This is a narrative description of the line items in your budget, with a detailed explanation for why you need each item and how you estimated the costs.

As a general rule of thumb, organize this document clearly, with headers, and follow the sequence of your budget. Proposal reviewers and program officers will read this alongside your budget spreadsheet. Leave no room for doubt about how you came to your cost estimates, and relate each expense to the methods and plan of work laid out in your proposal.

A word of caution: the budget justification is not the place to include additional information that you could not squeeze into your proposal. We have seen many attempts to add extra information about the methodology, for example, in the budget justification. Trying to do this will just add confusion and irritation for your reviewers.

Summary

Budgets are an important part of your proposal and cannot appear to be an afterthought or disengaged from the narrative portion. After all, asking for money is the whole point of writing a proposal. For this reason, your budget needs to be an integrated and compelling part of your overall story. Accuracy and thoroughness are critical to assuring reviewers that you have a solid plan.

Aside from the proposal sections discussed so far in this book, there are many other small sections and additional parts of a proposal to include, depending on the individual agency or program that you are applying to and the page limit of your proposal. We cover these in the next chapter.

Bibliography

National Science Foundation. (2016). *Report to the National Science Board on the National Science Foundation Merit Review Process, Fiscal Year 2015.* Recent reports can be found here: www.nsf.gov/nsb/publications

11

OTHER PROPOSAL SECTIONS

Beyond the key sections that we discussed in prior chapters, there are several additional parts that you will include in most proposals. Some of these are within the proposal narrative itself, and some are included separately as part of the overall package. In this chapter, we will give you some tips and strategies for the following proposal sections that will make every detail of your proposal shine:

- Timeline
- Dissemination plan
- Qualifications of the PI
- Letters of recommendation
- Citations and bibliography
- Data management plan
- Appendices

Timeline

Within the Methodology or Plan of Work section, or towards the end of your proposal, it is very useful to include a timeline or schedule of your research. This can be as simple as a chronological list if the research project is relatively short and simple, such as:

> July–September 2017: secondary source data collection and synthesis, home campus
>
> October–December 2017: archival data collection, French overseas archives, Aix-en-Provence
>
> January–June 2018: analysis of materials and drafting two journal manuscripts, home campus

Activity	Month											
	Jul	Aug	Sep	Oct	Nov	Dec	Jan	Feb	Mar	Apr	May	Jun
Create project webpage	X											
Collect & normalize existing data	X	X										
Develop interview instruments	X	X										
Field Work: Site A			X	X	X	X	X					
Field Work: Site B							X	X	X	X	X	
Data input			X	X	X	X	X	X	X	X	X	
Data processing and analysis					X	X	X	X	X	X	X	X
Writing and submitting publications									X	X	X	X
Meeting at scholarly conference												X
Evaluate project outcomes, write final report												X

FIGURE 11.1 Gantt Chart

If the project is more complicated, it is useful to lay out your plan of work in a Gantt chart in table format, showing the flow of work throughout the project, such as in Figure 11.1.

A timeline will allow the reviewer to see the overall scope of work in one place, and it will also assure them that your plan is well thought out and feasible.

Dissemination Plan

Usually placed toward the end of your proposal narrative, information about your dissemination plan will give the reviewer a sense of the more practical results of your research. What are the tangible outcomes or deliverables? In a longer format proposal, you might include a header for this section. But even for a short three-page proposal, include a line or two explaining:

- When and where you will publish your results (be specific about exact target journals and/or whether you have had preliminary conversations with a press).
- When and where you will present your findings (be specific about which conferences you will present at and when).
- Other media related to your research, whether it is a website, a policy briefing, a public database, a K-12 outreach program, or a museum exhibit. (Note that in an NSF proposal, this information would go specifically under your Broader Impacts section of the proposal.)

Qualifications of the Researcher or Team

Some RFPs request information about the investigator explicitly, but even if not required, this should be inserted strategically in your proposal. Include information that will highlight your strengths and simultaneously allay potential fears or hesitations among the reviewers. Are you conducting research in the Amazon forest? Then be sure to mention that you speak, for example, Yanomamö. Are you studying materials in the Egyptian archives? Then explain your expertise in reading hieroglyphics. In relation to field or archival work, and your methodology, this is a good opportunity to discuss your prior experience or arrangements at your research site.

- Do you have special training?
- Have you piloted your unique method?
- Have you studied in this location before?
- Do you have the proper permits?
- Have you made prior contacts?
- Have you collected preliminary data?

This can also be a good place to discuss your past accomplishments (books, journal articles, exhibits—and mention any awards for these if applicable) and how your current work builds on the prior work. If working with a team, discuss prior collaborations and evidence of success.

Letters of Recommendation

Several HSS grant and fellowship competitions require letters of recommendation. Graduate students and post-docs will be accustomed to this routine. But for faculty, you probably thought you were done with that when you applied for your last faculty position! Nope. Even for full professors with multiple grants under their belt, some agencies want to balance the reviewer evaluation of your proposal with the endorsement of your own colleagues and mentors. Requiring letters of recommendation can reduce the agency workload by weeding out a large number of unserious and unhoned proposals. This is because most faculty members won't submit something half-baked if they have to ask a colleague to write about it (and its author) in a letter. These recommendations also provide an additional layer of quality control for program officers when making final funding decisions.

The Guggenheim Fellowship application, for example, requires letters from:

> four persons who are familiar with your work and can comment on your abilities, especially in relation to your project proposal. Those who are familiar with your recent work and can comment on the course of your career as a whole will make the best references. Individuals who have a business or financial interest in your work—such as dealers, agents, and editors—would not be the most impartial references to provide, and would not be considered especially useful.

There are two main categories of letter writers whom you should court:

1. The famous star in your field
2. Your most ardent and supportive mentor and/or colleague

If you are lucky, 1 and 2 are the same people. If you are not so lucky, then swing to get as far to the fences as you possibly can. The point is that you want the reviewers and program officer to have some notion of who these recommenders are and why they should be trusted to pontificate on the brilliance of your proposal and career. As always, think about your audience! Who are the reviewers likely to be and from what fields? If you are applying for a National Endowment for the Humanities Fellowship (which requires two letters of recommendation), for example, don't ask a quantitative social scientist to write you a letter.

For the famous star in your field, you can't ask her to write you a letter if you don't know her. And you should have an established relationship with her as well—not just an awkward introduction at your national disciplinary conference two years ago. So if you can't get the star to write you a letter, go for someone senior and well known in your field or sub field. As for your supportive mentor or colleague, consider asking your department chair or your dissertation advisor or other colleagues and collaborators who you have collected along the way—again thinking through if this person will be a known and trusted entity at your agency.

For anyone whom you ask to write you a letter, make sure that they will write a *strong* and *detailed* letter. There tends to be a good amount of praise inflation in academic letters of recommendation. Given the increasingly stiff competition, and declining success rates for funding, your letters need to be enthusiastic, if not over-the-top passionate, about you and your contribution to your field. Lukewarm or succinct letters stand out to reviewers as they pore over their pile of proposals. An underwhelming letter of recommendation can be the kiss of death.

Citations and Bibliography

To cite or not to cite? This is a frequently asked question among humanities and social science proposal writers. And many agencies fail to give guidance about this topic in their RFPs. For the most part, we like citations, and we think you should use them in specific sections of your proposal to contextualize your research within your discipline or subfield. However, make sure to investigate the norms of your target agency and sample successful proposals to decide if citations make sense in your proposal.

Even the Bibliography section is a key strategic component of your proposal that you should write with care. Some reviewers go straight to your bibliography before reading the narrative for a preliminary overview of the content of your proposal. Whom you cite is a quick code for the theoretical and methodological foundations of your research and provides an important part of the overall story for the reviewer.

As we explained in prior chapters, your work should build on other research in your field. As you lay out the antecedents to your work and how your proposed research makes important contributions to your field, be sure to cite the key scholars in your area. These should include the representative seminal papers and books, up to the most recent and cutting-edge work that informs your project. For shorter format proposals (or in the cases where the bibliography is included in your total page count), this must be done deftly with only a few citations that you are sure your review panel will recognize as key works.

For longer format proposals where there are no limits on the bibliography, it is still important to edit your choice of citations judiciously. Reading a proposal that is choppy, with multiple citations after every sentence, can be distracting. You also don't want to give reviewers too many threads to follow or too many ways to critique your proposal. If you are going to cite someone, make sure it is not gratuitous—it should be closely integrated into the logic of your proposal.

As a general rule of thumb, your bibliography should only include work that you have cited in your proposal. However, some RFPs will ask for a bibliography as a guide to your knowledge and understanding of the field, regardless of whether you cite anyone in the proposal itself. The National Endowment for the Humanities Fellowship application, for example, includes this requirement:

> The bibliography should consist of primary and secondary sources that relate directly to the project. Include works that pertain to both the project's substance and its theoretical or methodological approaches. Evaluators will use the bibliography to assess your knowledge of the subject area.

A final take-away is to make sure you pay the correct homage to your potential reviewers through your bibliography. If you assume that the agency will choose reviewers who are experts in your field, don't offend them by neglecting to cite their work!

Data Management Plan

In the social sciences and humanities (digital humanities in particular), data management plans (DMPs) are becoming common components in proposal packages. Agencies want to know what kinds of data you are generating and how your data or materials will be made available for future use by other scholars or the public. A DMP is *not* the same as your human subjects protocol that you submit to your institutional review board (IRB). Although you might include parts of your IRB protocol in your DMP, the DMP is a broader document that is more geared to future storage and dissemination of your data. Many resources are available to help you write your DMP and subsequently fulfill the plan once your research is funded.

Because a DMP is required with every proposal submitted to the National Science Foundation, its Directorate for Social, Behavioral and Economic Sciences (SBE) has authored DMP guidance, which can be found here: www.nsf.gov/sbe/

sbe_data_management_plan.jsp. This document provides a succinct outline of the kinds of information that you should include, divided into the following categories:

- Expected data
- Period of data retention
- Data formats and dissemination
- Data storage and preservation of access
- Additional possible data management requirements

This is a great place to start in designing your DMP. But this format may not fit every humanities or social science proposal. Another great resource for help in designing your DMP is your campus library. Many university and college libraries now offer assistance with writing your DMP, in addition to having data storage, curation, and sharing services available in-house.

The University of California has developed the DMPTool, which includes sample DMPs, and an electronic wizard that assists you in designing and writing a DMP (https://dmptool.org/). Anyone can use this website; it is not restricted to University of California employees.

Libraries and other national organizations also host data repositories that can store, manage, and disburse your data through standardized and secure protocols. If your library does not have its own data storage and access system, the Interuniversity Consortium for Political and Social Research (ICPSR) is a leading data archive for the social sciences and beyond. Along with archive and access services, ICPSR offers educational workshops on data analysis. More information about them can be found here: www.icpsr.umich.edu/icpsrweb/index.jsp. You may also find data storage sites specific to your research topic, such as the Digital Archaeological Record (tDAR), for . . . you guessed it: digital records of archaeological investigations. In some instances, a funder will require that you submit your data to a special archive. The Registry of Research Data Repositories (re3data) is an excellent search engine of available datasets and repositories, with information and links for each (http://re3data.org/).

Be aware that data archiving might cost money, even if the service is at your home campus. Do research into these costs before writing your proposal so that you can include the expenses in your proposal budget.

Appendices

Appendices to a proposal might include a number of documents, such as:

- Data collection instruments (your interview questions, for example)
- Writing sample
- Descriptions of your institutional setting or facilities
- Collaboration plan (detailing roles and responsibilities for multi-investigator projects)

- Evaluation plan
- Work portfolio (applicable if your work involves museum exhibits, photography, documentary film, or other types of media)

We advise that you do not include any appendices with your proposal if they are not explicitly asked for. At worst, they could be considered nonconforming to the guidelines and might disqualify your proposal for review. If no appendices are required but you feel adamant that you should include something, check with your program officer first.

Summary

By the end of this chapter, you have all the information you need to compose a thorough and compelling grant or fellowship proposal! The sections covered in this chapter—from Gantt charts to data management plans—are not necessarily the most critical components of your proposal. Nevertheless, they will stand out if written poorly and cast a shadow on an otherwise excellent narrative. If well conceived and well written, these additional proposal sections will make your overall project shine. But you may still have some questions, such as:

- How do I find and work with a collaborator?
- What if my proposal is rejected?
- What happens if I get my grant?!

The final sections of this book will help you navigate these questions.

BOX 11.1   FLASH TOPIC: PROPOSALS FOR MEETINGS, BOOK COMPLETION, AND OTHER RESEARCH-RELATED ACTIVITIES

In the humanities and social sciences, we frequently need funds for research-related work, such as convening scholarly conferences and meetings, and finishing our book after all the research is completed. Here we show you how to find funds for these activities and key strategies for writing these types of proposals.

Meetings, Conferences, and Workshops

First, let's distinguish between two categories of conferences and meetings. On the one hand, you may want to present the findings of your research at your annual disciplinary organization meeting. Sometimes you can include funds for these types of conferences in your budget for research grants. More often, funds for this type of scholarly activity are available from your home campus or from your disciplinary organization. It is uncommon to find extramural grants and fellowships that will only fund your travel to attend a conference.

On the other hand, if you want to convene a scholarly conference, meeting, or workshop about a specific research topic, there are a handful of grants out there to help you accomplish this work.

Federal Funders

The National Endowment for the Humanities (NEH), the National Institutes of Health, and the National Science Foundation (NSF) have mechanisms for supporting conferences and workshops.

- At the **National Endowment for the Humanities (NEH)**, there are several grants to convene workshops, seminars, and other types of scholarly meetings. These include:
  - Institutes for Advanced Topics in the Digital Humanities
  - Landmarks of American History and Culture: Workshops for School Teachers
  - Public Humanities Projects
  - Summer Seminars and Institutes

  Each of these NEH opportunities has its own RFP and annual deadline. Study the details at the NEH website to determine if one of these might be a good fit for your project.
- The **National Institutes of Health (NIH)** funds conferences through its R13 mechanism. Your proposed conference should be closely aligned with the mission and program goals of the relevant NIH institute or center. For this reason, you must obtain permission to submit an R13 proposal from the appropriate scientific or research contact at your target institute or center. The majority of NIH institutes and centers accept conference grants in response to the Parent R13 Announcement, which comes out roughly every three years, with several proposal submission deadlines over multiple years.
- For programs in the **National Science Foundation (NSF)** Directorate for Social, Behavioral, and Economic Sciences (SBE), conference proposals should be submitted through the same process, and by the established deadlines, for each NSF program. Information about conference proposals can be found in the current NSF Proposal and Award Policies and Procedures Guide (PAPPG). Although it is not required, it is a best practice to consult with a program director before submitting a conference proposal

to NSF in order to gauge the fundability of your idea and a feasible ball-park budget.

Private Funders

Several foundations and private agencies also fund different types of scholarly meetings related to the specific interests and missions of the organization. Most of these are for relatively narrow disciplinary or topical areas:

- American Academy of Religion
- American Council of Learned Societies
- Association for Asian Studies, Inc.
- Chiang Ching-Kuo Foundation for International Scholarly Exchange
- International Society of Political Psychology
- Japan Foundation
- Mellon Foundation Sawyer Seminar
- Rockefeller Foundation Bellagio Center Conference Program
- Terra Foundation for American Art
- Wenner-Gren Foundation for Anthropological Research

Proposal Strategies

Writing a proposal to convene a conference or workshop follows many of the guidelines provided in this book. Do not make the mistake of envisioning your meeting as a salon to discuss your past publications or an established theme in your topic area. Like a research proposal, conference proposals should engage cutting-edge topics that make a significant contribution to the current state of knowledge in a given field. As such, conceptually build your conference or workshop proposal using strategies provided in prior chapters, including:

- Articulate the theoretical significance within the context of research in your field by using the common knowledge–disruptor pattern in your writing (see Chapters 5, 7, and 8).
- Strongly integrate your conference content and outcomes to the mission and objectives of the funding agency.
- Convey a solid plan through a well-designed conference program and related budget. You should include proposed dates, a list of speakers and participants, a complete conference agenda, and other sources of funding for the conference.
- Describe your administrative competence, or the resources provided by your institution, to manage the conference logistics. Does your campus have a Conference Services Office? Will your department staff handle

travel arrangements and printing? Can you point to past experience in facilitating group dynamics and agenda setting?

- Explain the outcomes of the conference or workshop in detail. These might include:
  - A new research agenda
  - A series of joint publications or an edited book
  - A multi-investigator proposal for a large grant
  - New curricula, courses, exhibits, or outreach programs
  - Training for new investigators in your field

In the HSS disciplines, funding to convene a conference will typically come from multiple sources, and in many cases will rely on individual participants paying their own way to attend. However, we find that seed funding from your campus goes a long way in igniting interest from extramural finders, or vice versa. Once your well-planned project has garnered core funding, you will likely receive more from other sources as the excitement spreads.

Book Completion and Long-Term Writing Projects

One of the principal complaints we hear from humanities and social science scholars is, "I don't need money, I need time!" Namely, time off from teaching and other campus responsibilities to write. Especially in the humanities and humanistic social sciences, where the end result of a research project is typically a book, several months or an entire year is needed. Finding funding specifically for writing is even harder to come by than funding for research.

Because it is extremely difficult to fund several months of your salary through a grant or fellowship (recall that the success rate for NEH fellowships is 6%), try to organize your larger writing projects around natural breaks in your academic career. For example, can you find funds to supplement your sabbatical leave? Can you compact your teaching load into one semester so that you can combine summer and a nonteaching semester into a longer block of productive writing time? And at the same time, don't forget the benefits of daily writing! These days, it is not realistic to leave projects unfinished until the perfect grant is won. Following is a selection of foundations and agencies that have grants for "buying out" time for writing projects for humanists and social scientists. Be sure to consult a funding search engine to seek a wider range of opportunities that may be available.

- American Association of University Women, American Fellowships
- American Council of Learned Societies (ACLS)
  - ACLS Fellowships
  - Henry Luce Foundation/ACLS Program in China Studies Postdoctoral Fellowship
  - Frederick Burkhardt Residential Fellowships for Recently Tenured Scholars

- National Endowment for the Humanities (NEH)
  - NEH Fellowship
  - NEH Summer Stipend
  - Scholarly Editions and Translations Grants
  - Awards for Faculty at Hispanic-Serving Institutions
  - Awards for Faculty at Historically Black Colleges and Universities
  - Awards for Faculty at Tribal Colleges and Universities
- John Simon Guggenheim Memorial Foundation Fellowship
- Woodrow Wilson National Fellowship Foundation
  - Mellon Career Enhancement Junior Faculty Fellowship
  - Mellon Career Enhancement Adjunct Faculty Fellowship

Visiting or Residential Fellowships

Apart from the grants that we list here, if you are willing to relocate for a year to do your writing (and/or research), many more opportunities are available. Visiting or residential fellowships are typically given for up to a year, and you are required to be in residence at the sponsoring institution, center, university, or library. Landing one of these grants will give you:

- The chance to temporarily break the ties at your home institution that can distract you from writing
- Access to materials or sites that you could not study at your home institution
- A valuable community of like-minded scholars in which to network and form new collaborations and mentor–mentee relationships
- Time and space to devote yourself full time to the completion of your book or other scholarly project

Residential grants typically fund travel and a monthly stipend, and they sometimes will also cover research expenses, basic relocation costs, and funds to support family members. In certain cases, you will be required to teach a course or contribute to the host community by giving a colloquium or seminar lecture, for example. Following is a selection of foundations and agencies that offer residential fellowships for humanists and social scientists, categorized as either domestic or foreign. Be sure to consult a funding search engine to seek a wider range of opportunities that may be available.

Domestic

- Amy Clampitt Residency Program in Poetry
- American Antiquarian Society, Fellowships
- Cornell University, Society for the Humanities, Senior Scholars in Residence Fellowships

- Emory University, James Weldon Johnson Institute for the Study of Race and Difference, Visiting Scholars
- Getty Foundation, Getty Scholars Grants
- Harvard University, Radcliffe Institute for Advanced Studies, Fellowship Program
- Huntington Library Fellowships, Long Term and Short Term Awards
- Institute for Advanced Study, Members
- Library of Congress Kluge Fellowships
- National Humanities Center Residential Fellowships
- Newberry Library Long Term and Short Term Fellowships
- Notre Dame Institute for Advanced Study, Residential Fellowship
- Russell Sage Foundation Visiting Scholars Program
- School for Advanced Research, Resident Scholars and Summer Scholars Programs (anthropology and related social science disciplines and the humanities)
- Stanford Humanities Center, Fellowships for External Faculty
- University of California Los Angeles, Visiting Scholar Fellowship Program in Ethnic Studies

Foreign

- Alexander von Humboldt Foundation, multiple fellowships (Germany)
- American Academy in Berlin, Fellows (Germany)
- American Academy in Rome, Rome Prize (Italy)
- Bogliasco Foundation, Fellows (Italy)
- Council of American Overseas Research Centers (multiple fellowships and locations)
- Fulbright Scholar Program, Core Teaching/Research Awards (multiple countries)
- German Academic Exchange Service (DAAD), Research Stays for University Academics and Scientists (Germany)
- Max Planck Institutes, International Visiting Researchers (Germany)
- Rockefeller Foundation Bellagio Residency Program (Italy)
- University of Cambridge, Centre for Research in the Arts, Humanities, and Social Sciences, Visiting Fellowships (England)
- European Research Council, various grants (to carry out research in the 28 EU Member States or associated countries)
- Netherlands Institute for Advanced Study in the Humanities and Social Sciences, Individual Fellowships (Netherlands)

Proposal Strategies

When writing a proposal for funding to complete your book or other large writing project, you should follow the guidelines in this book for constructing a successful proposal, in addition to providing ample information about the book and your progress to date. Here are some general tips for writing book proposals:

- Follow the guidelines in this book for writing the Introduction, Theoretical Significance, and Methodology sections—include all of these components in your book proposal even though this work is in the past. This information is necessary for reviewers to understand the scholarly contribution of your book and to be assured about the quality of your methods and analysis.
- Include a description of the overall format of the book, as well as brief descriptions of each and every chapter—even if the target grant will only fund the writing of a subset of chapters. Providing information about only a subset of chapters will be confusing to the reviewers.
- If additional research is required, be specific about the precise plan of research and how it fits into your overall writing schedule during the funding period. Also discuss if you have other grants or fellowships to pay for the various parts of the remaining project.
- Clearly explain your progress to date and timeline for completion.
- Include information about your publishing plan; if you are well into writing a book, you should have already considered the appropriate presses and have contacted the relevant editors. If applicable, mention which presses have expressed interest or if you have a contract in place.

BOX 11.2 PROPOSAL EXCERPT: BOOK COMPLETION PROPOSAL SAMPLE FROM A PROPOSAL TO THE NATIONAL ENDOWMENT FOR THE HUMANITIES FELLOWSHIP PROGRAM

Title: Lady First: Sarah Childress Polk and the Wages of Womanhood

Author: Amy Greenberg, PhD, History

The following proposal section is the final portion of a successful proposal to the National Endowment for the Humanities. The first sections of the proposal (not included here) cover the research question, theoretical context and significance, methods, and analysis. These final paragraphs explain details of the qualifications of the author, a sequential explanation of each chapter of the book project (with headers), and how the NEH fellowship will enable the successful completion of the important project.

I am in a unique position to tell the intersecting story of Sarah Childress Polk and women's political activism in the mid-nineteenth century. I have published four books on the politics of the antebellum era, including the leading examination of the relationship between changing gender norms and the ideology of Manifest Destiny, *Manifest Manhood and the Antebellum American Empire* (Cambridge, 2005). While writing my trade book, the prize-winning *A Wicked War: Polk, Clay, Lincoln, and the 1846 U.S. Invasion of Mexico* (Knopf, 2012, Vintage paperback edition 2013), I proposed that the U.S.-Mexican War should be known as Mr. and Mrs. Polk's War, and offered a portrait of a politically-savvy First Lady that many readers found compelling and controversial. Indeed one of the most frequent questions I received when delivering over thirty public lectures about the U.S.-Mexican War over the past four years is whether I intended to write a biography of Mrs. Polk.

I have been exceptionally fortunate to gain the assistance of archivists at the main repositories of Sarah Childress Polk's manuscripts and material collections. The curator of the Polk House and Museum, Tom Price, has shared materials with me that have not previously been considered by a biographer, editors of the Polk Correspondence at the University of Tennessee have given me access to unpublished material, and the editor of the Madison Papers has provided me with a cache of previously unused letters between Dolley Madison and Sarah Polk that illuminate the extent of their remarkable relationship. Thanks to an archivist at Salem College (Childress Polk's alma mater), I've had the opportunity to examine a previously unknown letter between Sarah and her father, the only such letter in existence.

I expect this biography will gain a wide readership among scholars and students of nineteenth-century gender and women's partisan politics. Because my subject is a First Lady, there is reason to believe the book will also find an audience among those interested in presidential history, as well as those Americans interested in the role of women in the White House, past and present. By synthesizing decades of scholarly research into an archive-based narrative biography, this project will promote the understanding and appreciation of the humanities among the general public.

Table of Contents

Introduction: The introduction contrasts Sarah Childress Polk and Elizabeth Cady Stanton, two political women whose experiences overlapped in numerous ways, but whose historical fortunes were remarkably different. Polk was immensely famous in the 1840s, and even more powerful than she was famous. But she was forgotten by 1870. Stanton yearned for power in the 1840s, and grew more famous over time. This contrast reveals that a governing narrative of expanding American democracy has obscured how political power was exercised in the past. Sarah Polk's experience reveals a hidden history of women shaping high politics before "earning" the vote.

Chapter One: "Blackboard, Maps, and Globes". The chapter begins with a portrait of Sarah's family, community, and religion, in Murfreesboro, Tennessee, focusing in particular on the constraints facing women in the early nineteenth century, as well as the importance of territorial expansion to the financial success of slave-holding families like the Childresses and Polks. But Sarah's early years are not simply marked by constraint. She is surrounded by political men who recognize her intelligence, and unique educational opportunities open her eyes to the possibilities of the wider world. When her father dies she returns home from boarding school in North Carolina, and although only fifteen is forced to face many of the responsibilities of adult womanhood, including caring for her grieving mother and her younger siblings. Like countless other young women in the Early American Republic, the teenaged Sarah Childress longs for autonomy and self-actualization. Many women found a road to freedom through evangelical religion: supporting temperance and abolitionism on the road to Woman's Rights. Sarah follows a different path, embracing the conservative Democratic political milieu in which she was raised. At age twenty she marries a young state legislator named James K. Polk. Sarah, James, and their slaves move into a small cottage on the larger Polk property. Her mother-in-law does all the entertaining, which frees her from the normal responsibilities of a young wife. Because James underwent experimental surgery for bladder stones as a teenager he can't father a child. James lifts the weight of their childlessness by integrating Sarah into his political life.

Chapter Two: A Salon in Washington [writing sample]. At Sarah's urging, James successfully runs for Congress, and although it defies convention, she follows her husband to Washington. She thrives in the intensely political atmosphere of Washington, and turns her boarding house into a political salon. While scholars have argued that women's involvement in partisan politics was limited in the first half of the nineteenth century, women largely structured Washington DC political life, and much of Sarah's early power derives from her ability to manipulate a network of powerful political spouses. When James wins the post of Speaker of the House, Sarah takes on extra rooms for the purposes of entertaining, and presides over social events that are dominated by men. She thus becomes the first Washington wife to successfully integrate the worlds of male and female gossip.

Chapter Three: State Politics. James returns to Tennessee to run for governor, and Sarah becomes his campaign manager. During his three campaigns he becomes increasingly dependent on Sarah for political information. "You must send me news," he repeatedly writes, asking her to lobby various editors and politicians. But her ability to live up to his expectations is compromised by her responsibilities to her household. Her struggle to balance the demands of home and what both she and James consider her real "work" of politics force the couple to openly reevaluate conventional gender roles: he doesn't care if she ignores the domestic as long as she is proficient in politics. As First Lady of Tennessee Sarah takes on clear and recognized authority among state politicians. James' political allies back in Washington also miss her. Three different men write her letters complaining that without her help they are no longer able to obtain "information" in the manner they used to.

Chapter Four: "That All Your Actions May Be Original". James successfully runs for president in 1844, with Sarah as campaign coordinator. One of the first things they do once in the White House is set up a shared office in the domestic quarters. Dolley Madison mentors Sarah in how to use the domestic powers of the First Lady to best advantage. But Sarah surpasses her mentor in her manipulation of her public image. Sarah's announcement that she will not be redecorating the White House, as had previous first ladies, reveals her genius at public relations. The public embraces her for her thrift and good sense, but in fact leaving the White House in its current somewhat dilapidated space spares her the work of redecorating. Sarah leaves the hard work of "visiting," normally the biggest time-sink for a Washington political wife, to the two nieces who live with them in the White House. This allowed Sarah to focus her energies on advancing James' agenda to expand the boundaries of the nation to the Pacific. She controls his access to news, and the access of other politicians to him. She also takes over the management of their family plantation. She also attempts to tame his workaholism. Never strong in constitution, James fades under the stresses of running a war.

Chapter Five: Neutral Ground. When James K. Polk dies three months after leaving office in 1849, he makes Sarah executor of their estate, and leaves their plantation in her hands. A grieving and devastated Sarah takes control of their plantation and is forced, for the first time, to operate independently. At the start of the Civil War Sarah deploys the "wages of womanhood" and refuses to take a loyalty oath to either the nation, or the Confederacy. She asserts, and is able to maintain, that Polk Place is neutral ground, revealing the extent to which her political skills are still useful as a widow. All of her actions further the Confederate cause, some in what could be considered treasonous ways, yet the Union respects her autonomy. She entertains both Union and Confederate generals at Polk Place, and after the war successfully wins damages from the U.S. government for destruction of her property in Mississippi.

Chapter Six: About Relics. Sarah survives forty-two years as a widow, but never leaves Nashville. The final decades of her life are spent entertaining visiting dignitaries and working assiduously, but unsuccessfully, to redeem James K. Polk's memory. Polk's reputation disintegrates during Reconstruction, and the U.S.-Mexican War he fought is largely forgotten. Yet up until her death in 1891, Sarah continues to uphold patriotism over personal scruples, publically asserting that the war was right, and that regardless of considerations of international law or morality, she was "in favor of" any actions that "helped strengthen the United States." Her final resting place in the Polk tomb is fitting. Her domestic identity provided her with surprising power and authority during James' life, but its constraints only became apparent after his death. Her comments to visitors during the last decade of her life reveal the extent to which she already envisioned herself entombed by his side. At the same time, her legacy lives on in the actions of her niece and nephew, who are instrumental in "redeeming" Tennessee from the Republican Party during Reconstruction. Her niece takes Sarah's place as first lady of Tennessee during the first Democratic governorship after the Civil War. And her nephew helps found the Ku Klux Klan in Pulaski.

Epilogue. This volume ends with an evaluation of Sarah's relationship to both the early struggle for women's rights, and the origins of female conservative activism. Sarah never recognizes the extent to which the feminists were right, but her embrace of the Woman's Christian Temperance Organization in her final decade, suggests that she has finally accepted the need for women to lead. It's no coincidence that the only reform organization she ever joined began as an intensely conservative one. The WCTU has been recognized by scholars as a landmark organization, the first national vehicle for female conservative activism. By revealing Sarah Childress Polk's contribution to the origins of the WCTU, her place in the origin story that ultimately leads to both the modern female conservative movement, and a female American presidency, becomes clear.

Work Plan: I have currently completed the first three chapters of this project, an introduction, and the conclusion, as well as the research for the remaining three chapters. A NEH Public Scholars Fellowship will allow me to devote a solid year, beginning September 2016, to completing my final three chapters. The attached letter from Knopf attests to their plan to publish the book in 2018 with an initial hardcover print run of 8,500 to 10,000 copies, to be followed a year later with a Vintage Books paperback edition. Based on Knopf's launch of *A Wicked War* I expect to embark on a multi-city public speaking tour in support of the book, to conduct a large number of radio interviews and podcasts, and for the book to be reviewed in mainstream newspapers and periodicals. Once published, *Lady First* will challenge contemporary perceptions about female political power, and provide a new origin story for the history of women in American presidential politics.

PART III
Working With Others

12

INTERDISCIPLINARY AND COLLABORATIVE RESEARCH

Working alone has long been the norm in the humanities and social sciences. More recently, however, collaborative research within and across the disciplines has become more common. Our increasingly networked society is rapidly opening new access to information and expertise and new ways of addressing social and cultural problems. There is also growing recognition that science and technology are embedded in social relationships and cultural practices, and funding agencies are in turn interested in approaches that take what is called a SHTEAM approach (Science, Humanities, Technology, Engineering, Arts, and Math).

For the purposes of this book we will use the terms interdisciplinary, multidisciplinary, team science, and collaborative somewhat interchangeably, although we acknowledge the differences between them: interdisciplinarity generally refers to working across the methods and material of two or more disciplines within a project—reflecting the idea that complex problems are best addressed and understood by an integrated approach. Multidisciplinary work is characterized by groups of co-researchers who have identified a common research question they feel might be best addressed by multiple coordinated approaches—explicitly questioning the disciplinary status quo.

Regardless of what you call it, we have seen a steady increase in funding opportunities for collaborative research in recent years. However, don't jump on this bandwagon just because it is the rising trend! You should engage in collaboration because it makes sense for your research goals and those of your prospective collaborators. In this chapter we will describe the current funding trends for collaboration in the humanities and social sciences and offer best practices for forming and managing successful partnerships.

Institutional Support for Interdisciplinary and Collaborative Work

If you are considering embarking on a new collaborative or interdisciplinary project, it is important for you to have a clear sense of the culture of support for this kind of work within your institution. We can look to Arizona State University

(ASU) as one example of how an institution has reorganized *itself* in response to new research and teaching trends. At ASU, the campus is organized into units such as the School for the Future of Innovation in Society and the School of Sustainability. The overarching goal is to establish innovative relationships to address the most pressing issues of the 21st century—specifically through interdisciplinarity and collaborative work.

If you are not situated within an institution that has radically rethought the traditional landscape of academic schools and departments, you should nevertheless identify the spaces on your campus that promote and facilitate interdisciplinarity. Look for centers, interdisciplinary programs, or specialized schools outside of your home discipline and department. If you can't find an existing organization that meets your interests, start your own. Initiate a reading group, for example, or discuss the possibility of establishing a new cross-campus network or center with like-minded colleagues.

At the same time, weigh your interdisciplinary inclinations against the requirements for completing your dissertation or gaining tenure and promotion. Talk to your mentors and colleagues about how collaboration and interdisciplinarity fit into the arc of your career. Generally speaking, the dissertation and pre-tenure years are not the best time to jump into collaborative projects. These projects take more time and energy to navigate and manage, and the results might not meet your need to produce what is necessary for your promotion case or degree. For example, how many sole-authored publications (or first-author or last-author) are required for a slam dunk tenure case? Are you expected to publish only in the leading journals in your discipline, or will interdisciplinary journals also count? How does your department account for your contributions to co-authored articles?

That is not to say that you should ignore collaboration altogether before tenure! Start building collaborative relationships as early as possible; they are key to longer-term funding options and scholarly productivity in an academic career. Dip a toe into a collaborative project and participate in limited ways if it does not impede on the work you need to do alone for tenure. Research on co-authorship patterns illustrates that collaborative research yields more funding, more citations, and higher-impact scholarship than individual projects (Wuchty, Jones & Uzzi 2007; Stokols, Hall, Taylor, & Moser 2008; Uzzi, Mukherjee, Stringer, & Jones 2013). Better recognition and rewards for interdisciplinary collaboration is on the horizon. More and more universities are adopting tenure and promotion policies that value teaming, and this trend is growing.

Funding Trends

The majority of funding for collaborative humanities and social science scholarship tends to fall into three categories:

- Research
- Publications
- Academic conferences or gatherings

However, alternative outcomes to collaborative work are increasingly being supported by academic funders, particularly in relation to public scholarship; partnerships with communities and nonprofits; and collaborations that span STEM, social sciences, humanities, and the arts.

Federal and State Funders

The National Endowment for the Humanities (NEH) funds projects that involve bringing large datasets online, collaboratively written series, and multiformat endeavors that include outputs as diverse as websites, books, public programming, and even roadside signage. Some examples of NEH opportunities for collaboration include:

- Collaborative Research Grants
- Common Heritage
- Creating Humanities Communities
- Dialogues on the Experience of War
- Digging into Data Challenge
- Digital Humanities Grants
- Humanities Access Grants
- Humanities Initiatives Grants
- Public Humanities Projects
- Summer Seminars and Institutes

The National Science Foundation (NSF) has multiple opportunities for collaborative research. For each program in the NSF Directorate of Social, Behavioral, and Economic Sciences (SBE), you have the option of submitting a collaborative proposal with multiple investigators and institutions through the regular annual grant competitions. If your collaborative research project falls across multiple programs or directorates, you can request—or a program officer can request—that your proposal be reviewed by multiple programs, and thus could be funded jointly. In addition, NSF holds specific competitions for grants that are required to be interdisciplinary, often involving several NSF directorates. Often referred to as "Crosscutting" programs, some examples are:

- ADVANCE: Increasing the Participation and Advancement of Women in Academic Science and Engineering Careers
- Cultivating Cultures for Ethical STEM (CCE STEM)
- Inclusion across the Nation of Communities of Learners of Underrepresented Discoverers in Engineering and Science (NSF INCLUDES)
- Innovations at the Nexus of Food, Energy and Water Systems (INFEWS)
- National Science Foundation Research Traineeship (NRT) Program
- Partnerships for International Research and Education (PIRE)
- Research Coordination Networks
- Science and Technology Centers: Integrative Partnerships

Note also that the NSF frequently signals an inclination to fund interdisciplinary research through "Dear Colleague Letters." These are not RFPs, per se, with dedicated funds. Instead they typically encourage proposals on specific interdisciplinary topics to be funded through the standard existing programs at NSF. Examples of recent "Dear Colleague Letters" for the Social Sciences include "Enabling New Collaborations between Computer and Information Science & Engineering and Social, Behavioral and Economic Sciences Research" and "Opportunities for Research in Smart & Connected Communities."

The National Institutes of Health (NIH) allows applicants and their institutions to identify more than one principal investigator (PI) on a single grant application for the majority of their grant types. As an alternative to the traditional model of a single PI, their goal in creating this option is to encourage collaboration among equals when that is the most appropriate way to address a scientific problem. The NIH also has several grant opportunities that require interdisciplinary collaboration. Some examples of these involving social and behavioral sciences are:

- International Research Collaboration on Drug Abuse and Addiction Research (R21)
- International Research Collaboration on Alcohol and Alcoholism (U01)
- Predictive Multiscale Models for Biomedical, Biological, Behavioral, Environmental and Clinical Research (U01)
- Systems Science and Health in the Behavioral and Social Sciences (R21)

A handful of other federal agencies have specific collaborative funding opportunities that could involve humanities and social science researchers. They include:

- *Department of Defense (DOD)*
  - Multidisciplinary University Research Initiative (MURI). Topics change annually. Recent examples that involve social sciences include:
    - Cyber Deception through Active Leverage of Adversaries' Cognition Process
    - Media Analytics for Developing and Testing Theories of Social Structure and Interaction
    - Novel Approaches to Modeling Factions and Conflict
    - Network Science of Teams
- *Department of Education (ED), Institute for Education Sciences (IES)*
  - Partnerships and Collaborations Focused on Problems of Practice or Policy Grants Program (Research Collaborations Program)
  - Research Networks Focused on Critical Problems of Education Policy and Practice (Networks)
- *Department of Transportation (DOT)*
  - University Transportation Centers (UTC) Program
- *National Oceanic and Atmospheric Administration (NOAA)*
  - Climate Program Office, Climate and Societal Interactions Program

At the state level, there are fifty-six nonprofit state and jurisdictional humanities councils, many of which also lean toward supporting work that is highly collaborative or that places traditional humanities scholarship into conversation with a wider array of contemporary topics and issues.

Private Funders

The following is a selection of private foundations and agencies that have funding opportunities explicitly for collaborative, multi-investigator research in the humanities and social sciences:

- American Council of Learned Societies (ACLS), Collaborative Research Fellowship
- American Council of Learned Societies (ACLS), Robert H. N. Ho Family Foundation Collaborative Research Fellowships in Buddhist Studies
- Russell Sage Foundation Visiting Scholars Program for Collaborative Groups
- U.S.-Israel Binational Science Foundation, Regular Research Grants
- Wenner-Gren Foundation, International Collaborative Research Grants

Proposal Strategies

Do the research to understand funders' priorities and what they hope to get out of their investment in you and your collaborative project. The American Council for Learned Societies, for instance, wants their collaborative research grants to result in a co-authored academic publication. The National Endowment for the Humanities, on the other hand, funds a much broader scope of activities ranging from publication to digital archives and databases, to archaeological excavation, analysis, interpretation, and more. No matter the funding agency, pay special attention to the following areas in your collaborative proposal and submission process.

Proposal Writing Leadership and Coordination

Collaborative proposal writing often takes much longer than an individually authored proposal. With two or more writers involved, there are additional rounds of review and editing to allow each collaborator to make their mark. Several meetings, whether in person or virtual, should punctuate the writing of the proposal. It can be difficult to schedule these among busy people, especially across time zones, which can also extend the timeline for preparing the proposal.

Throughout this process, it is mandatory to designate a lead writer; someone who is given license to bring disparate proposal parts together and make final editorial decisions as the deadline approaches. Make sure to use a cloud sharing platform, such as Google Docs, Dropbox, or Box, to simplify the co-writing and editing process.

Proposal Submission Logistics

It is important to be aware of timelines within your own institution and your partners' institutions when putting together a collaborative proposal. Your department or Sponsored Projects Office staff will need additional time to coordinate collaborative agreements, subcontracts, and integrated budgets, for example.

Translate Disciplinary Language

With interdisciplinary and collaborative proposals, it is especially important to anticipate who your reviewers might be. Before writing a proposal, you and your partners need to decode disciplinary language and concepts as you develop your research project. Translate key terms in your proposal to ensure that reviewers from any of the disciplines involved in your research will understand them.

Underscore the Interdisciplinary Contribution

If you are collaborating, there must be a critical topical, theoretical, or methodological alchemy that will make a significant contribution to the areas of research in which you are jointly engaged. Do not expect reviewers to grasp this without your guidance. Be explicit in your writing about the nature of the collaboration, the precise ways that you are bringing disciplines together, and why your collaborative approach yields benefits beyond what one discipline or researcher alone could have produced.

Describe the Partnership

Clearly describe the partners, their complementary expertise, and precise roles and responsibilities in the research. Address why the partners chosen are the most appropriate to achieve the end goals of the project. If applicable, mention past collaboration and results; reviewers might feel more comfortable funding a proven collaborative team.

Create a Management Plan

Include a convincing management plan in your proposal, whether or not it is required. If the proposal is funded, it can serve as a great guide for research teams throughout the course of the grant. Specify shared or hierarchical leadership structures, when and how you will meet and communicate to keep the project on track (weekly teleconferences, for example), and the timeline for milestones and deliverables.

The Dating Game: How to Find the Right Collaborator

The most successful and productive collaborative research projects develop naturally out of preexisting relationships. These can be formed through various types of interactions on or off your campus, such as committees, shared lab or office space, professional conferences, or through the extended networks of your mentors, colleagues, and students. Research on teams illustrates that longer-term relationships that include nonwork social interactions are the most conducive to strong and trusting teams (Huber & Lewis 2010; Pentland 2012). Studies also suggest that geographic proximity creates more robust teams, as more frequent face-to-face personal encounters build the trust and familiarity that are critical to effective teamwork (Pan, Kaski & Fortunato 2012; Onal Vural, Dahlander & George 2013).

Thus, based on both the research on teams and our own experiences in and among research teams, we don't advocate the "blind date" approach to research collaborations. Yet sometimes it is the only way to form a team in quick response to a new and exciting funding opportunity. How do you identify and solicit collaborators either from across your own campus or external to your institution? Networking is not easy for all academics, but it can pay off in eventual research collaborations. Start on your campus or in your university system and ask for suggestions from colleagues. Alternatively, some funding search engines have built-in scholar profile databases that allow you to search nationally and internationally for potential collaborators by topic area. In these blind date situations, proceed with caution, and do your best to vet your prospective collaborator before getting too deep into the relationship.

A better approach is to stay abreast of funding trends in your areas of research, review the published strategic plans of your target funding agencies, try to get invited to agency advisory committees, and establish a good relationship with relevant program officers. In this way, you can anticipate—if not help to shape—the future directions of interdisciplinary humanities and social science research. If you have insights into an up-and-coming collaborative research opportunity, work with your campus Research Development office or divisional leaders to convene a campus mini-symposium to allow potential collaborators to share their research and discover connections. By putting in this proactive work, you can already have the networks and teams in place to take advantage of funding opportunities that emerge.

Here are some concrete steps you can take to start forming a research team, whether it is arranged hastily or a longer-term process:

- After gauging the interest of prospective collaborators on a specific idea or funding opportunity, have a face-to-face meeting for agenda setting and vision sharing—if not in person, at least by video-conference.
- Create an environment where all voices are heard and where each person has an opportunity to contribute to the overall concept. If the proposal doesn't shape up to represent the research interests of each of the partners, momentum and trust may be difficult to sustain.
- Don't become—or don't invite—the "token" team member. Many recent RFPs are requiring broad interdisciplinary collaboration, such as engineering and arts, or society and STEM. Particularly for those of us in the humanities and social sciences, make sure that your team appreciates the value of your discipline in the overall research project. Your work should be thoroughly

integrated into the project and not just an afterthought or appendage to get the larger project funded.

- If time allows, look for seed funding for your project to test the waters with your team. Seed funding might pay for an in-person meeting or pilot data collection, for example.
- Consider the benefits of building a *diverse* team. Apart from the innovation that results from colliding disciplines, several studies suggest that including gender, national, and racial-ethnic diversity are beneficial to team performance, innovation, and productivity (Woolley, Chabris, Pentland, Hashmi, & Malone 2010; Campbell, Mehtani, Dozier, & Rinehart 2013; Freeman & Huang 2014).
- Discuss publication goals as part of the proposal development process. As you build the research project and related division of labor, make sure that each member will accomplish what they need from the collaboration, namely publications—but this might include other products. Think through how the research questions and data collection will lead to an array of publications and a situation where each team member can have the lead or last-author role in a journal that will benefit their next promotion case.

Effective Team Leadership and Management

Research teams tend to fall along a continuum between two types: goal driven or exploratory. Goal-driven teams might be working towards a grant proposal deadline or working on a project that has hard deliverables and milestones. These tend to benefit from hierarchy, defined roles, and strong leadership. Exploratory teams have a more flat organizational structure, in which roles are less defined and decision making is consensus based. This type of team is more common at the outset of research collaboration, when ideas are still percolating towards a solid proposal idea. Most teams cycle through both goal-driven and exploratory periods, depending on the project they are working on or the phase of a given project.

What does this mean for collaborative proposal writing and research? Because the majority of research-related teaming is goal driven, *leadership* is very important. It is advantageous to have one strong leader for the project who can maintain the overall vision and keep the moving parts on track. If you plan to lead a collaborative team, be aware that it takes a significant amount of additional time to manage work progress and team communication. You should be highly organized and have the ability to pleasantly "nag" people to meet deadlines. You might also be called in to sort out sensitive interpersonal relationships. If this role does not sound appealing to you, we don't recommend leading a research team.

If you are a junior faculty member, think twice about taking on this kind of commitment, especially before you have tenure. The additional time needed to manage teams will detract from the time you have to produce the articles or book that you need for your tenure or promotion case. Also as a junior faculty member or graduate student, carefully scrutinize the leadership structure of any team that you are invited to join. Make sure that the project is in the hands of a competent and experienced leader.

Some excellent tools are available to help you build and manage collaborations, and we provide a list of resources in Chapter 15. Some of the best advice includes:

- Be prepared for disagreements and conflicts with strategies for how to manage these. These are a natural part of a successful teaming process (Tuckman 1965; Tuckman & Jensen 1977). As graduate students and faculty members, we do not traditionally receive instruction in interpersonal communication and conflict resolution as part of our academic training. Seek out basic team management courses at your campus business school or other local organizations that offer these.
- Set expectations and responsibilities early (the NIH has developed a comprehensive set of questions for collaborators to ask before embarking on a project, often referred to as the "team science pre-nuptial agreement": https://ccrod. cancer.gov/confluence/display/NIHOMBUD/Collaborative+Agreement+Te mplate).
- Facilitate effective meetings and communication. Establish rules for interaction that will limit "air time hogs" and interrupters. Reduce status difference by making sure that everyone is heard. If certain members are not adding to the discussion, be sure to explicitly ask them frequently for their input.
- Build and maintain team trust. Be a reliable team member in the work arena, and find opportunities for your team to interact outside of the work environment. Identify and emphasize team values and goals. Build on this "superordinate identity" by making coffee mugs for all team members, or a poster in your research lab, that displays your project name or a meaningful or humorous quote that relates to your work.

Fifty Ways to Leave Your Lover—When Collaborations Go Awry

Sometimes, teams fall apart. This is often the result of failing to do the upfront work required to assemble and maintain a successful team. If you find yourself on a team that is failing, or worse, exploding, you might consider various ways of confronting team members or withdrawing from the team. There might be fifty ways to leave your lover, but extracting yourself from research collaborations is much more complicated! "Slipping out the back, Jack" usually doesn't work because there is a lot at stake, and you must consider carefully:

- The commitments you made to the team and funding agency in terms of your expertise or connections to data, field sites, or samples
- Losing access to jointly collected data and/or co-authorship on publications and other products that will result from the research
- How your reputation might be affected by exiting from a project or by taking a conflict to higher and more visible levels, such as the funding agency, journal editorial boards, or campus general counsel

Our advice is to try to find ways to work through the conflict. Your campus ombudsperson might be able to offer ways of understanding the source of the problems and effectively addressing them. The Team Science Field Guide also offers several resources for solving conflicts on academic teams (Bennett, Gadlin & Levine-Finley 2010). However, this is sensitive territory in academia, and conflict resolution strategies might be considered too "touchy-feely" for some of your collaborators. Recognize also that a set of interrelated power structures is in place that may prevent you from adequately solving conflicts. There is a large body of literature that inventories the myriad ways in which junior faculty members, women, underrepresented minorities, and others with intersectional and diverse identities are subject to implicit biases, micro-aggressions, and discrimination in the higher education environment (Gurin, Dey, Hurtado, & Gurin 2002; Mitchneck, Smith & Latimer 2016).

If you are still faced with insurmountable conflict after trying the leadership, management, and conflict resolution tools listed earlier, find ways to divide the work and funding to separate specific team members and thus circumvent the conflict, even if not solving it. Reconfigure the project so that tumultuous relationships can be side-stepped and problematic tasks can be allocated to different people or accomplished in different ways. This is not ideal team science or collaboration, but might salvage the funding, the research, and your reputation in the meantime.

Summary

Forging collaborative research partnerships may be a big step out of the comfort zone for many humanists and social scientists. Don't collaborate just because it is trendy or required by the funding agency. Collaborate because you have genuine curiosity about how your research can be transformed by different perspectives, methods, or analyses. Opportunities for collaborative and interdisciplinary research are growing by the year. But be cautious about the timing of collaboration in the arc of your career. Collaboration, particularly if you are leading it, can be enormously time intensive. There are many resources and strategies for developing strong and productive research teams and managing their complexity over the life of the project. Whereas this chapter has focused on collaboration on academic teams, next we turn to collaborating with community partners and the public in Chapter 14.

Bibliography

Bennett, L. M., Gadlin, H., & Levine-Finley, S. (2010). *Collaboration & Team Science: A Field Guide*. NIH Office of the Ombudsman, Center for Cooperative Resolution.

Campbell, L. G., Mehtani, S., Dozier, M. E., & Rinehart, J. (2013). Gender-heterogeneous working groups produce higher quality science. *PLoS ONE, 8*(10), e79147.

Freeman, R. B., & Huang, W. (2014). *Collaborating With People Like Me: Ethnic Co-Authorship Within the US* (No. w19905). National Bureau of Economic Research.

Gurin, P., Dey, E., Hurtado, S., & Gurin, G. (2002). Diversity and higher education: Theory and impact on educational outcomes. *Harvard Educational Review, 72*(3), 330–367.

Huber, G. P., & Lewis, K. (2010). Cross-understanding: Implications for group cognition and performance. *Academy of Management Review, 35*(1), 6–26.

Mitchneck, B., Smith, J. L., & Latimer, M. (2016). A recipe for change: Creating a more inclusive academy. *Science, 352*(6282), 148–149.

Onal Vural, M., Dahlander, L., & George, G. (2013). Collaborative benefits and coordination costs: Learning and capability development in science. *Strategic Entrepreneurship Journal, 7*(2), 122–137.

Pan, R. K., Kaski, K., & Fortunato, S. (2012). World citation and collaboration networks: Uncovering the role of geography in science. *Scientific Reports, 2*, 902.

Pentland, A. (2012). The new science of building great teams. *Harvard Business Review, 90*(4), 60–69.

Stokols, D., Hall, K. L., Taylor, B. K., & Moser, R. P. (2008). The science of team science: Overview of the field and introduction to the supplement. *American Journal of Preventive Medicine, 35*(2), S77–S89.

Tuckman, B. W. (1965). Developmental sequence in small groups. *Psychological Bulletin, 63*, 384–399.

Tuckman, B. W., & Jensen, M. A. (1977). Stages of small-group development revisited. *Group and Organization Studies, 2*, 419–427.

Uzzi, B., Mukherjee, S., Stringer, M., & Jones, B. (2013). Atypical combinations and scientific impact. *Science, 342*(6157), 468–472.

Woolley, A. W., Chabris, C. F., Pentland, A., Hashmi, N., & Malone, T. W. (2010). Evidence for a collective intelligence factor in the performance of human groups. *Science, 330*(6004), 686–688.

Wuchty, S., Jones, B. F., & Uzzi, B. (2007). The increasing dominance of teams in production of knowledge. *Science, 316*(5827), 1036–1039.

13

FUNDING FOR PUBLIC SCHOLARSHIP

Public scholarship, also known as community-engaged research, engages higher education faculty in advancing the public and civic purposes of humanities, arts, and social sciences. By collaborating with—and making research accessible to—community partners, scholars can make a tangible difference in the world. In doing so, they are designing innovative models, methodologies, and languages for scholarship and integrating research with exciting teaching and community service approaches. Public research and scholarship are also becoming accepted modes of achieving tenure and promotion. This chapter will explore current trends in public scholarship and identify and discuss specific sources and strategies for funding these kinds of projects.

Current Trends in Public Scholarship

Although colleges and universities have long recognized the value in outreach programs, and in fact include them as an integral part of the public mission of the teaching institution, outreach has frequently been defined by a one-way relationship where the university offers a specific resource to the community. Conventional outreach programs include everything from adult education, internships, on-campus programs for young learners, and events and curricula that bring university expertise into K-12 classrooms. It is likely that your institution has one or more offices devoted to outreach or educational partnerships. If you are considering doing this kind of work, these existing departments are a good place to begin networking to formulate a project and funding plan.

Recently, however, a new dialogue has emerged around the practice of university-community engagement, as both scholars and community groups have sought to develop new language for what this kind of work can and should accomplish. More recent "town and gown" relationships address important civic topics and involve interdisciplinary teams of scholarly and community experts. These collaborations have scholarly outcomes in the form of data collection and journal articles, for example, that go hand in hand with practical outcomes such as policy recommendations, museum exhibits, workshops for at-risk populations, or documentary films.

We emphasize throughout this book that your research project must have scholarly significance, be rigorously grounded in existing literature, and make an important theoretical contribution to your field. However, this is not necessarily the model that should guide your proposals for public scholarship and community-engaged research. Your proposal for this type of project should certainly be informed by current theories and methods in your field, but most funders of public scholarship and community-engaged research will want the focus to be squarely on the practical and societal outcomes of the project. If the project allows you to make an important theoretical advance, that is great! But this is not how you sell it to potential funders.

If you are a scholar who wants to engage the public, whether it is local, regional, or national, you must begin to ask questions such as:

- Who decides what the relevant issues are?
- Who designs the approach to address these issues?
- Whom does the scholarship serve?
- Who benefits from the research and how?

One key element that differentiates public scholarship from more traditional outreach models is recognition that the community can be much more than a laboratory for, or recipient of, university service and research. Your partners should be considered equals, who are integrated into a project from the first steps, including conceptualizing the project, developing the research questions, participating in data collection and analysis, co-producing the results and deliverables, sharing resources, and getting credit along with their university partners throughout.

Where to Begin?

A good place to begin thinking about your contribution to public scholarship is with the national consortium Imagining America: Artists and Scholars in Public Life (http://imaginingamerica.org/). They provide an excellent overview of what public scholarship looks like across a wide range of institutions nationally.

Imagining America has also addressed important questions about how publicly engaged scholarship is received and assessed by institutions of higher education in their Tenure Team Initiative work (see Chapter 15 for links to their materials). Before launching into public scholarship, it is important for you to consider how this fits into the arc of your academic career and the extent to which it will be recognized and rewarded by your department and institution. Although there is growing recognition of the legitimacy of public scholarship, it may not "count" among your peers, particularly prior to getting tenure.

If you don't already have strong partnerships with the community you want to collaborate with, don't despair—meeting people is the easy part! Begin by identifying community leaders and introduce yourself. Be prepared to spend some time listening to their ideas about what the community wants, needs, and is interested in. Volunteer with relevant organizations to understand the environment, and offer your expertise in their ongoing initiatives. Don't expect them to understand or even support your research right away; trust, mutual respect, and shared goals take time to develop.

As with academic collaborations discussed in Chapter 12, setting equitable expectations and responsibilities prior to beginning a project is critical. The National Institutes of Health Office of the Ombudsman Partnering Agreement Template is a good place to start (https://ccrod.cancer.gov/confluence/display/NIHOMBUD/Collaborative+Agreement+Template), but with community collaborations additional questions should be posed. These include:

- How do scholars and community members define and value each other's knowledge and expertise?
- What counts as data, evidence, and methods by different stakeholders?
- How can findings be interpreted in multiple ways by different stakeholders?
- Are university human subjects protocols acceptable to the community participants and vice versa?
- How does the project build community capacity, empowerment, and sustainability?

The Current Landscape for Public Scholarship

Funding for public scholarship and community-engaged research is often highly project specific. In other words, it will be rare to find a funder who casts a broad net for projects that are simply community engaged. Rather, you and your partners will need to do a bit more searching for the right funding fit.

Local community foundations are a good place to start. They usually have a stated interest in investing in the local area and addressing specific, preidentified areas of need. Even if your project does not directly map onto their stated goals, a conversation with a program officer will clarify how they might support your work or lead to additional possibilities for project funding that were previously not on your radar.

When approaching local community foundations, don't hesitate to start with a small funding request that will allow you to do some preliminary research, test and establish your partnership, or pilot a small portion of the program you envision. Some agencies will indicate that they are interested in funding the start-up phase of a project, such as a planning grant. After your program is initiated or scoped out successfully, the same funder may renew or expand your funding. At the same time, you can turn to additional funders to implement various parts of the project. Consider breaking up funding requests into distinct pieces—a curricular/learning component might find funding from on-campus resources; the community action pieces may each appeal to local 501(c)(3) funders; and the academic research with wider policy implications could garner funding from a national foundation or agency. Don't forget to align each of your requests to the funder's priorities: if your local community foundation is interested in alleviating hunger or engaging children in early learning experiences, be sure to indicate how your research will shed new light on these issues in your community and how your partnership will work to address them in the real world.

It's a Partnership: Who Should Apply for the Funding?

Several of the funders listed next are expressly interested in funding nonprofit or community groups. If you call a program officer and explain that you are a university researcher, they may tell you they don't support academic work. Although a longer conversation about your community-engaged research might be useful, it is often more expedient to have your community partner be the initial applicant for the funds to avoid confusion. If your community partner is a nonprofit organization with 501(c)(3) status, they are generally eligible to apply to foundations. Always read the request for proposals and FAQs for each opportunity closely: often there is a minimum annual operating budget or requirement for number of years in existence that must be met.

If your partner does not have 501(c)(3) status and it is not appropriate for you to apply through your college or university, you can explore fiscal sponsorship for the project through a local or national umbrella organization. These organizations have a clear process and timeline for this procedure, so be sure to allow sufficient time to meet this eligibility requirement. Further information about the costs and benefits of fiscal sponsorship, as well as advice about how to find one, can be found at Grant Space, which is a service of the Foundation Center: http://grantspace.org/tools/knowledge-base/Individual-Grantseekers/Fiscal-Sponsorship/fiscal-sponsorship.

Working With Your Campus Development Office

You should coordinate your outreach to foundations and private funders with your Campus Development Office (sometimes called institutional advancement). For the most part, the Development Office (not to be confused with the *Research Development* Office which focuses on funding for faculty research) is largely in the business of doing more general fundraising for campus buildings and infrastructure, large programmatic initiatives, student scholarships, and endowed professor programs, for example. Faculty research is not their priority; however, it is a great idea to talk to them when you are making your plans for public scholarship and community-engaged research.

Most university development offices have strong relationships with various higher education–related foundations and private funders. Some development offices have staff dedicated to these relationships. They can help you understand the mission of specific funders and perhaps help you get an appointment with a relevant program officer at an agency. At the same time, it is important that you don't accidentally step on the toes of an ongoing relationship between your campus and a foundation. A useful decision-making guide is as follows:

- If a private foundation has a published request for proposals (RFP) for a specific funding opportunity, proceed with your application, but let someone at your Development Office know in the event that they have contacts at the foundation that might be beneficial.
- If you find a foundation that does not have a published RFP, but you think they might be interested in your work, contact your Development Office first and ask them for advice in initiating the conversation. Cold-calling a foundation will get you nowhere. In many cases, foundations deal with unsolicited funding requests from the public through a letter of intent or letter of inquiry (LOI) process. Very rarely does an LOI result in funding. You will have a much better chance if someone at your Campus Development Office can help you make a personal connection.
- If your Development Office does not have a contact at your target foundation, they may offer to assist you in contacting the appropriate person. Also, you can study what organizations the foundation has funded. If they have funded universities or scholars in the past, contact the scholar whom they have funded to ask for advice about how they were able to build the relationship and if they can provide contact information for the program officer who funded their community-engaged research. You might not always get help through this route, but it is worth a sincere try!

Funding for Public Scholarship

The terrain for public scholarship funding is rapidly changing as the civic responsibility, and applied aspects, of higher education come more into focus nationally. Table 13.1 provides a selection of current opportunities for public scholarship and community-engaged research, but be sure to consult a funding search engine to seek a wider range of opportunities that fit your specific project.

Crowdfunding

If you can't find a funding opportunity specifically for your area of community-engaged work or public scholarship, crowdfunding can be an excellent alternative. We give detailed advice for developing and running a crowdfunding campaign earlier in this book in Flash Topic 2.1. A fundamental component of successful crowdfunding is developing and engaging an audience around your project. Your community-based partners may already have large networks of supporters or stakeholders, as well as relationships with other organizations that can help disseminate your campaign. Even if you don't specifically partner with a community-based

TABLE 13.1 Selected Funding Opportunities for Public Scholarship and Community-Engaged Research

Agency and Program	Topic Areas Funded
American Association of University Women (AAUW) Community Action Grants	Research projects that promote education and equality for women and girls
American Council of Learned Societies (ACLS) Public Fellows Program	Places recent PhDs in two-year staff positions at partnering organizations in government and the nonprofit sector. This program aims to expand the reach of doctoral education in the United States by demonstrating that the capacities developed in the advanced study of the humanities have wide application, both within and beyond the academy.
Bringing Theory to Practice, Campus Dialogue Grants	Facilitates the greater purposes of higher education: learning and discovery, well-being, civic engagement, and preparation for living meaningfully in the world.
Knight Foundation	Journalism and arts.
Kresge Foundation	Arts and culture, education, environment, health, human services.
National Archives and Records Administration, Public Engagement with Historical Records	Access to America's historical records to encourage understanding of our democracy, history, and culture.
National Endowment for the Arts (NEA), Creative Placemaking Grants, Our Town Initiative	Creative placemaking projects that help to transform communities into lively, beautiful, and resilient places with the arts at their core.
National Endowment for the Humanities (NEH) Creating Humanities Communities	Makes connections between organizations that will foster community cohesion on a local or regional level, to stimulate and proliferate meaningful humanities activities in states and U.S. territories underserved by NEH's grant-making divisions and offices
National Endowment for the Humanities (NEH) Dialogues in the Experience of War	Supports the study and discussion of important humanities sources about war in the belief that these sources can help U.S. military veterans and others to think more deeply about the issues raised by war and military service.
National Endowment for the Humanities (NEH) Humanities Access Grants	Capacity building for humanities programs that benefit one or more of the following groups: youth, communities of color, and economically disadvantaged populations.
National Endowment for the Humanities (NEH) Humanities Connections	Expands the role of the humanities in the undergraduate curriculum at two- and four-year institutions, focusing on connecting the resources and perspectives of the humanities to students' broader educational and professional goals, regardless of their path of study.

(Continued)

TABLE 13.1 (Continued)

Agency and Program	Topic Areas Funded
National Science Foundation (NSF) Advancing Informal STEM Learning (AISL) program	Advances new approaches to the design and development of STEM learning opportunities for the public in informal environments, provides multiple pathways for broadening access to and engagement in STEM learning experiences, and advances innovative research on and assessment of STEM learning in informal environments.
Rockefeller Brothers Fund	Democratic practice, peace building, sustainable development.
Shelley and Donald Rubin Foundation	Art and social justice.
Sociological Initiatives Foundation	Supports research that furthers social change, including social policy, institutional and educational practices, linguistic issues (e.g., literacy, language loss and maintenance, language policy), and community capacity and the organization of previously unorganized groups.
Sundance Documentary Fund	Nonfiction cinematic documentaries on contemporary themes.
Surdna Foundation	Sustainable environments, strong local economies, thriving cultures.
U.S. Department of Justice (DOJ), Community Policing Development Grants	Advances the practice of community policing through training and technical assistance, the development of innovative community policing strategies, applied research, guidebooks, and best practices that are national in scope.
Wenner-Gren Engaged Anthropology Grant	Enables Wenner-Gren grantees to return to their research locale to share their research results with the community in which the research was conducted and/or the academic/anthropological community in the region or country of research.

organization, your project can attract support from other interest groups or online communities that are involved in your topic.

For example, in 2011, Dr. Kristina Killgrove (a biological anthropologist currently at the University of West Florida) launched a crowdfunding campaign to conduct research on skeletons from burial grounds near Rome, Italy. As recounted by Jai Ranganathan on the #SciFund Challenge website (https://scifundchallenge.org/), Kristina had been blogging about anthropology since 2007 (www.poweredbyosteons.org/). She also had over 2,500 connections via Twitter and Google Plus. By blogging for years about her topic, Kristina learned effective ways of explaining anthropology in a compelling way to people who might not know much about the field. The audience following her blog had recently grown after she began writing reviews of the TV show *Bones* (a cop show that revolves around forensic anthropology).

When developing her crowdfunding campaign, Kristina focused on three target audiences: a) people interested in anthropology, b) people interested in Ancient Rome and in the Classics more broadly, and c) the general public. Apart from writing about her crowdfunding campaign on her blog, Twitter, and Google Plus accounts, she also posted an article on the Ancient Rome section of the social news website Reddit. News of her project spread through these communities, and it was eventually featured in the CNN blog post "Light Years." A fourth audience for her work emerged through this publicity: "weekend genealogists." Varying her messages for her public audiences was critical to her success. For some audiences, pitching the project as research into the forgotten 99% of Ancient Rome was a winning message. For other audiences, the Latin angle was effective. In less than two weeks, Kristina had received over $9,000, surpassing her original goal of $6,000. By the end of the four-week campaign, she had received a total of $12,331.

Kristina's experience also underscores how public scholarship can advance your career in exciting ways. A *Forbes Magazine* editor covered her crowdfunding campaign in 2011, and when he was subsequently looking to expand his stable of science writers in 2015, he remembered Kristina and gave her a platform. She is now a regular contributor at *Forbes* and Mental Floss (www.forbes.com/sites/kristinakillgrove/). This has given her more opportunities to connect with the public and earn money.

Summary

Public or community-engaged scholarship can be the most rewarding work in your academic career. Many of us would like to have our research have impacts beyond the Ivory Tower. Unless you are at a particularly progressive institution, however, it is advisable to achieve tenure before diving into public scholarship. Working with community partners, as with any collaborators, is a time-consuming undertaking. It is important to understand the ethics of community-engaged scholarship and to keep equity in mind from the outset to the end of your project. All parties should be engaged in the formation and results of the shared project.

Above all, as you think through how to fund your collaborative project, be thoughtful in devising a plan that does not impinge on, or compete with, the existing funding stream for your partner organizations. As with the collaborative project itself, the funding scheme for it should be complementary and integrated with your partner's ongoing activities and should ultimately serve their broader purpose and goals.

PART IV

From Failure to Funding

14

FAILURE OR SUCCESS

What Next?

You have spent months planning your project, refining your ideas, and writing the proposal. You have spent several more months waiting with bated breath for word from the funding agency. The day of reckoning finally arrives. Whether you are successful or not, the next phase in your proposed research project has begun. Let's start with the Unhappy Ending scenario.

Rejection

The rejection letter or e-mail message arrives, and a series of distressing emotions takes over:

> "All that work for nothing!"
> "I hate my job!"
> "The (your target funding agency inserted here) sucks!"
> "I am a loser!"

Let it all out. These feelings are normal, and you are not alone. If you haven't come to realize it yet, failure is simply part of your job. In academia, between faculty positions, journal articles, grants, and other indicators of success, *no one* is successful 100% of the time. In fact, we are rarely successful 30% of the time! Academia is, in fact, largely a life of rejection. Better to acknowledge this early on.

After taking a moment . . . or several days . . . to regroup, it is time to think through your next steps. What do you do next? You put a huge amount of effort into the process, and it's natural to be disappointed. But don't let this be your stopping point. As any seasoned grant-getter will tell you, multiple submissions are not uncommon before reaching success. We know a very successful full professor who submitted a proposal seven times . . . yes, SEVEN times! . . . to the National Endowment for the Humanities before finally winning an NEH fellowship. According to recent data for National Science Foundation grants, success is most common after 2.4 submissions. The lesson here is don't give up! The fact remains that you still have a need for funding for your project, and you have already put a lot of work into it. There is a series of things you can do to turn your failure into success.

Get Feedback on Your Proposal

Many agencies will send a summary of panel or reviewer feedback along with your rejection letter. This might consist of a brief analysis of the relative strengths and weaknesses of your proposal in relation to what they were looking for in a funded project. Although it may be your first instinct to fire off an e-mail demanding an appeal, because you know how strong your proposal was, for example, or because the reviewers did not seem to understand what a perfect fit it was for their agency, don't do it! It is much better to approach this as a learning opportunity and see the rejection letter as an invitation for a constructive conversation with the program officer. This is the person who has the greatest knowledge of the funding institution and should be familiar with your proposal and how it fits or doesn't fit within their institutional priorities. It is also likely that they were present during the reviewers' discussion of your proposal and will have special insight into how it was received and what the perceived weaknesses and areas of strength were.

The best course of action is to prepare a careful e-mail thanking your program officer for their communication and asking for an appointment for a phone conversation. Some program officers may not have the time to talk on the phone with every prospective or rejected applicant. If this is the case, ask if they can either send you more substantive written comments from the evaluation process or summarize the panel's responses for you in such a way that you can use them to improve the shape of your proposal. At other funding agencies, the program officer may be able to provide you with much more detailed information, advice, and even reapplication strategies. If you are invited to have this kind of conversation, please remember that this is not the time to convince the program officer of the merits of your application. Rather, spend your time listening and asking questions about how the committee responded to your ideas and what could be improved.

Although you may be focused on asking the questions about what was lacking in your proposal—don't forget to ask for an assessment of its strengths as well. When revising and resubmitting, the last thing you want to do is accidentally cut the piece that spoke most strongly to the reviewers. You may even be able to expand on these strengths in important ways.

It is also helpful to send your rejected proposal and the reviewer comments to a trusted colleague in your field and the research development professionals on your campus. They will have a more objective view of the critique and can help you distill the main points and the ways that you can revise your proposal accordingly.

It is frequently the case that proposal *writing*, instead of proposal *content*, is to blame for a rejection. If you come away from reading your reviewer comments thinking, "They didn't read my proposal carefully! They missed the whole point!" this is a sign that you did not write the proposal in a way that easily conveyed "the whole point." It is easy to accuse proposal reviewers of being sloppy readers, and indeed it is very often true. But remember what we discussed in Chapter 3: proposal readers do not spend hours and hours doing a close reading of your proposal. They have a stack of thirty or more to get through and will not take the time to decipher the true meaning of an opaque proposal.

Will the Same People Review My Proposal Next Time?

If you decide to revise your proposal and resubmit it to the same funding agency (and we strongly suggest you do), it is best to do so sooner rather than later. It can be strategic to have the same reviewers in the next round who remember your first attempt and see how you have improved it in response to their comments. Many agencies and foundations have rotating portions of their review panels serve for multiple years, and thus some members of the panel will remember your proposal. Reviewers like to know that you took their comments seriously and that you acted on their suggestions.

Whether or not the reviewers are new to your proposal, we often encourage proposal writers to include language in revised proposals that alludes to how you made improvements in response to reviewer comments on a prior submission. The National Institutes of Health requires such a statement describing the revisions in a resubmitted proposal. But for any agency, especially if your proposal received relatively positive reviews and encouragement for resubmission, you should subtly let reviewers know this in your resubmission. For example, at the end of your Introduction section, you might add a couple of sentences, such as:

> Based on the encouraging reviewer comments on my prior submission, I have carefully revised the project. In particular, I responded to excellent suggestions from reviewers in strengthening my methodological approach, and I have included references to recommended studies that provide a broader context for the significance of my research.

Was It All Just a Waste of Time?

You may ask yourself this question, but remember, a proposal is not wasted effort, even if you do not immediately get the funding. You now have a draft that you can revise and resubmit. You have suggestions for improvement from experts in your field. You can also use your rejected proposal as the basis for new proposals to other funding agencies. You have taken the time to crystallize your ideas and needs, and although you may need to describe them in different ways for other funding opportunities, the core of your next proposal is already written. If you have been involved in a collaborative proposal, you are well on your way to having a coherent and trusting team that is poised for the next opportunity that arises.

From Failure to Success: An Example

Isla Vista Arts is a hybrid interdisciplinary program at UC Santa Barbara that brings together teaching in departments across the humanities and fine arts with real-life production and publication experiences for students who enroll in the courses. Students produce a number of off-campus arts and culture events and experiences for their peers, including weekly live comedy shows and feature film showings, visual arts exhibitions and festivals, Shakespeare in the park, an arts and culture magazine, public murals, and more—all with the intent of using their growing academic expertise in the arts and humanities to revitalize their own local community (www. ihc.ucsb.edu/ivarts/).

After looking at funding opportunities, discussing joint interests, and assessing the institution's capacity to support such an expansion, a core interdisciplinary team of faculty and staff assembled a proposal for a National Endowment for the Humanities (NEH) special projects grant (no longer offered by the agency). A few months later we learned that although the proposal was highly regarded by reviewers, it was not ultimately funded. Reviewer comments echoed what we already suspected—that a panel of humanities experts had difficulty understanding how community-engaged arts research and practice fit within traditional definitions of the humanities. They wanted to believe that it could, but in the end felt there wasn't a strong enough humanities focus to warrant funding the large, multiyear project.

The work put into the proposal, however, set the stage for a longer-term campus commitment that now sustains this multifaceted program. The process of writing the initial proposal helped faculty and staff find ways the program could profitably expand (which it has), as well as sparked new ways of thinking about sustainable funding streams (campus lock-in fees and admissions charges, ad sales, ticket sales, longer-term commitments of campus support, and other grants). The high-profile nature of the initial proposal, and the kinds of campus commitments that were made in support of it, meant that key administrators had become keenly aware of the program and were in fact champions of its success; they were ready to continue to commit campus resources even when the proposal was not funded. Years later, the Isla Vista Arts program is still going strong.

Success

Now for the Happy Ending scenario: the program officer just called to tell you that you have been awarded your grant or fellowship! Time for the happy dance! Take out that champagne that has been chilling for the last several months and celebrate! As the euphoria wears off, it is time to start implementing your project.

Be aware that sometimes as the euphoria wears off, you realize the enormous scale and volume of the project that you proposed, and you start to panic. For many proposal writers, there might be a little remorse along with the joy. Because now you actually have to *do* all that work that you ambitiously laid out in that brilliant proposal. In many ways, grants and fellowships can be life changing, sending you off on momentous academic and geographic journeys into the great unknown. Although you might be anxious, don't fear! Your proposal itself is a step-by-step manifesto to guide your way into and through your project. Your plan is great! It has been vetted by discerning reviewers, and they found the project feasible, compelling, and a contribution to your field. Print out the timeline or Gantt chart that you included in the proposal and pin it to your bulletin board. Let it be your guide. You have planned out the work in great detail in your excellent proposal. Now you just have to "work the plan."

Institutional Support

After calling your mother to tell her the good news, start alerting the relevant offices and staff at your institution. Do you have collaborators? They will want to embark on the same process at their campus. Here is a handy checklist of whom you might need to talk to about your new grant:

- Agency program officer. (Some agencies make a personal phone call to tell you the good news of your success; others will send an e-mail. In the latter case, reach out to your program officer by phone to say thank you and ask about the next steps in the process.)
- Department chair
- Dean (even if the project does not involve her or his approval for things such as matching funds, course release, etc., why not toot your horn a little!)
- Grant manager (departmental or institutional)
- Sponsored Projects Office and/or Office of Research
- Collaborators
- Students who are being paid from the grant
- Contacts at research sites
- Mentors and colleagues who helped you with the proposal

In the meantime, the funding agency will likely be in touch with the appropriate offices at your campus to begin the process of routing the funds to the institution.

Note that if you received a fellowship that comes directly to you, you can expect a check in the mail or an electronic transfer. If you are planning to accept the fellowship as an individual, meet with your tax advisor to understand the tax implications of this award. If there is a way to route the funds through your institution, talk to your Sponsored Projects Office or Development Office about the process.

Human Subjects and Other Compliance Approvals

In the humanities and social sciences, we are not usually responsible for the many compliance issues that accompany "hard" science and engineering projects such as biohazards, vertebrate animals protocols, invention disclosures, and export controls. The main compliance issue that humanists and social scientists face is human subjects. Your campus will certainly have an institutional review board (IRB) that reviews and approves research protocols involving living human beings. If you are at a very small institution that does not convene a standing IRB, or if you are an independent scholar, the Department of Health and Human Services and the National Institutes of Health have online resources to locate an appropriate IRB for your project (see Chapter 15 for more information).

Juggling Multiple Grants

For many projects in the humanities and social sciences, funding is so paltry that we need multiple sources to complete an entire project. At the same time, there is an exponential growth curve to grant getting. Robert Merton coined the term the "Matthew effect" to describe how well-known scientists tend to get more credit than less well-known scientists for the same achievements (Merton 1968). The same effect seems to be true with grants and fellowships. The more funding you have under your belt (assuming you carry out the projects successfully and publish or produce other scholarly products accordingly), the more you are seen by agencies and reviewers as a good bet, and you will certainly have an edge over your competitors who are less experienced.

As such, there will be many times in your career that you will be juggling multiple sources of funding, whether they be grants, fellowships, or gifts. Many agencies require you to report current and pending funding in your proposal. In some cases you will need to negotiate with agencies about duplicate funding. Certain agencies will not allow you to have more than their fellowship for a given project, or they might put limits on the overall amount of funding you can have. The American Council of Learned Societies (ACLS), for example, states that "[a]n ACLS Fellowship may be held concurrently with other fellowships and grants and any sabbatical pay, up to an amount equal to the candidate's current academic year salary." In other cases, agencies allow you to have duplicate grants for the same project, but they will want justification for how you will spend their funds in relation to the other funding.

In any of these cases, it is important to communicate with your program officer. Be transparent about the funding you have, and justify why you need all of it. If you are in the lucky position of getting multiple grants for the same project, think of ways you can lengthen, expand, or improve the project with the additional funding, and make the case to the program officers that it will be money well spent. If you are faced with the decision of choosing one grant over another, think through the trade-offs between money and prestige. Sometimes, a smaller grant from a more prestigious agency might be the better choice in your longer-term career. In these situations, regardless of which grant or fellowship you choose, make sure to list all of them on your CV, with the notation "(declined)" after the name and amount of the award that you decided not to take.

When it comes to managing multiple grants, make sure to stay organized, and keep careful records of what each source paid for. You will need to report this in detail in annual or more frequent reports to the agencies. Hopefully, your grant manager at your institution can separate the funds into different accounts and produce spreadsheets that document precise expenditures for you.

Reporting

The agency will dictate the content and frequency of reports that you will need to submit during the grant period. In many cases they will provide forms or web portals to collect the desired information. Our main advice for reporting is to start early and keep meticulous records of your expenditures. Do not wait until the night before the due date to start working on your report. You will probably need to get financial information from your institution, and the funding agency will want substantive information about your progress to date. This includes an explanation of the work that has been accomplished, as well as an inventory of publications, presentations, student training, and other scholarly products. Reporting is also an opportunity to describe challenges and setbacks and the ways that you have overcome them or redirected the project. After submitting a report, don't be surprised if your program officer contacts you to ask questions or request more information.

Take reporting seriously. This is another form of evidence to a program officer that you are a reliable investigator, and prompt and thorough reporting can be a key piece of maintaining a good relationship with them. Many agencies will not accept future proposals from investigators who have outstanding reports to be filed.

When Things Don't Go as Planned

We emphasize throughout this book that proposal writing is fiction writing. No research project unfolds exactly as planned in the original proposal. In fact, you should always expect change, disruption, and contingency, and agencies expect this. Your campus grant manager or Sponsored Projects Office can help you decide when it is necessary to ask permission for budget adjustments from your agency program officer. Generally speaking, federal agencies allow for budget reallocations between categories of up to 10% of the total grant amount. Private funders have different thresholds. If, for example, you want to redirect 25% of the grant funds from student assistance to travel, write to your program officer with justification and ask for permission to proceed. Small adjustments, such as flights or equipment costing slightly more than you had budgeted, can be made without notifying the agency.

Apart from the budget, keep your program officer informed when there are major changes to the scope of the project. We can't give you precise guidelines for what is considered a major change by every agency. But if you feel that your project is moving in a new or different direction, it is better to reach out to your program officer early. They will let you know their expectations and tolerance for mission creep in your project. If things go awry, don't be afraid to let your agency know. As long as you are diligently carrying out your work and you have a viable solution to overcoming challenges or managing change, you will likely receive positive guidance and support from your program officer.

If, by the end of your grant period, your project is incomplete, you can request a no-cost extension (NCE), regardless of whether you have funding left over. Many agencies will automatically grant up to one year of NCE, and in certain circumstances you will be able to extend the grant period even longer.

Summary

Writing your proposal and submitting it is only a relatively small precursor to your eventual research project. Whether your proposal is rejected or funded, this moment is a doorway to the next phase of your project. This chapter has provided you with concrete steps to take in either situation. As you become more experienced with your research and proposal writing, you will see that proposal writing becomes routine in the ongoing spectrum of your research career. One project will lead to another (or several others), and your various research interests will converge and spin off into different projects throughout your career.

Reference

Merton, R. (1968). The Matthew effect in science. *Science, 159,* 56–63.

15

RESOURCES

We hope that this book has been useful in getting you started with proposal writing in the humanities and social sciences. In this chapter we inventory a variety of resources that can help you with additional information on topics that we have referred to throughout this book. They are listed by category in alphabetical order.

Bibliography of Other Great Proposal Writing and Research Development Books and Articles

Booth, W. C. & Colomb, G. G. (2016). *The Craft of Research, fourth edition*. Chicago: University of Chicago Press.

Gillis, C. (1993). *Strategies for Writing Persuasive Proposals in the Humanities*. Berkeley: Doreen B. Townsend Center for the Humanities.

Gillis, C. (2008). *Writing Proposals for ACLS Fellowship Competitions*. American Council of Learned Societies, www.acls.org/uploadedfiles/publications/programs/writing_fellowship_proposals.pdf

Heath, C. & Heath, D. (2007). *Made to Stick: Why Some Ideas Survive and Others Die*. New York: Random House.

Licklider, M. M. (2012). *Grant Seeking in Higher Education: Strategies and Tools for College Faculty*. San Francisco, CA: John Wiley & Sons.

Pzreworski, A. & Salomon, F. (1995). *On the Art of Writing Proposals*. Social Science Research Council, www.ssrc.org/publications/view/7A9CB4F4-815F-DE11-BD80-001CC477EC70/

Schimel, J. (2012). *Writing Science: How to Write Papers that Get Cited and Proposals that Get Funded*. New York: Oxford University Press.

Shore, A. R. & Carfora, J. M. (2010). *The Art of Funding and Implementing Ideas: A Guide to Proposal Development and Project Management*. Thousand Oaks, CA: SAGE Publications.

Watts, M. (2001). *The Holy Grail: In Pursuit of the Dissertation Proposal*. Berkeley: Institute for International Studies, http://iis.berkeley.edu/node/304; http://iis.berkeley.edu/sites/default/files/pdf/inpursuitofphd.pdf

Budget Examples

Following is a list of sample budgets and other resources available on funding agency websites. A web search for "sample research budget" or "sample research budget justification" will also yield many more examples for you to consider.

Sample Budget for the American Council of Learned Societies Robert H. N. Ho Family Foundation Program in Buddhist Studies: www.acls.org/uploadedFiles/Fellowships_and_Grants/Competitions/1314_SampleBudget_Ho_Coll.pdf

Sample Budget for The Wenner-Gren Foundation: www.wennergren.org/sites/default/files/Sample_Budget_Post_PhD.pdf

National Institutes of Health Guide to Developing Your Budget: http://grants.nih.gov/grants/developing_budget.htm

Collaboration and Team Science

The COALESCE Project (online learning resources to enhance skills needed to perform transdisciplinary, team-based translational research): www.teamscience.net/

Collaboration Success Wizard: (online diagnostic survey for geographically distributed collaborations) http://hana.ics.uci.edu/wizard/

Falk-Krzesinski, H. J. & Kim, B. Y. (2012). Guidance for team science leaders: Tools you can use. *BRAIN*, 2(1–2012), https://academicexecutives.elsevier.com/articles/guidance-team-science-leaders-tools-you-can-use.

Learning Team Collaboration Survey – This survey is intended to help teams learn about their current collaborative practices and goals for collaboration (developed for educators but can be modified for other groups): www.aea267.k12.ia.us/system/assets/uploads/files/380/learningteamcollaborationsurvey.pdf

NIH Collaborative Agreement Template: https://ccrod.cancer.gov/confluence/display/NIHOMBUD/Collaborative+Agreement+Template

Team Science and Collaboration Field Guide: https://ccrod.cancer.gov/confluence/display/NIHOMBUD/Home

NIH Team Science Toolkit: www.teamsciencetoolkit.cancer.gov/Public/Home.aspx

The Toolbox Project provides a philosophical yet practical enhancement to cross-disciplinary, collaborative science. Toolbox workshops enable cross-disciplinary collaborators to engage in a structured dialogue about their research assumptions, http://toolbox-project.org/Project –

Crowdfunding

#SciFund Challenge: http://scifundchallenge.org/

Crowdfunding and the Arts: https://ucsota.wordpress.com/2011/10/20/crowdfunding-and-the-arts-ucira-interviews-thuy-tran-of-united-states-artists-usa-steve-lambert-jeff-crouse-and-dan-froot-ucla-part-1/

Institutional Review Boards and Human Subjects

U.S. Department of Health & Human Services: www.hhs.gov/ohrp/

National Institutes of Health: https://humansubjects.nih.gov/

National Science Foundation and the National Institutes for Health: Agency-Specific Proposal Writing Guides

Together, the National Science Foundation and the National Institutes for Health fund around $35 billion in research grants each year. The National Science Foundation alone provides over 60% of the federal funding for basic research at academic institutions in the social, behavioral, and economic sciences. More than 80% of the NIH's funding is awarded through almost 50,000 competitive grants to more than 430,000 researchers. As such, several proposal writing guidebooks have been written that focus specifically on these agencies. If you are applying to either, it is well worth the investment to purchase and study one or more of these books. The agencies themselves also provide some guidance on their websites. Some examples are:

Gerin W., Kapelewski, C. H., Itinger, J. B., & Spruill, T. M. (2010). *Writing the NIH Grant Proposal: A Step-by-Step Guide*. Los Angeles: Sage.

The Grant Application Writer's Workbook: National Institutes of Health Version. Los Olivos, CA: Grant Writers' Seminars and Workshops LLC, www.grantcentral.com/workbooks/

The Grant Application Writer's Workbook: National Science Foundation—Fastlane. Los Olivos, CA: Grant Writers' Seminars and Workshops LLC, www.grantcentral.com/workbooks/

Yang, O. (2012). *Effective Grant Writing: How to Write a Successful NIH Grant Application*. New York: Springer.

NIH Office of Extramural Research Grants Process Overview: http://grants1.nih.gov/grants/grants_process.htm

National Institute of Allergy and Infectious Diseases, All about Grants: Tutorials and Samples: www.niaid.nih.gov/researchfunding/grant/Pages/aag.aspx

The National Science Foundation has one online proposal writing guidebook authored by the staff of the Division of Undergraduate Education (DUE), and as such focuses on this division. But it has relevancy across the directorates at NSF: www.nsf.gov/publications/pub_summ.jsp?ods_key=nsf04016

Public Scholarship

Imagining America: http://imaginingamerica.org/wp-content/uploads/2015/09/JHaft-Trend-Paper.pdf

Imagining America Tenure Team Initiative: http://imaginingamerica.org/initiatives/tenure-promotion/

Research Development

Many institutions have an in-house Research Development Office, often located centrally in the campus Office of Research, but sometimes within individual colleges or divisions. Research development professionals offer a range of services to investigators, from funding searches, to strategic proposal review, to building and managing collaboration teams. The profession grew exponentially during the

2008–2014 economic downturn as many institutions realized that more support was needed to generate competitive proposals in a tightening funding landscape. In 2010, the National Organization of Research Development Professionals (NORDP) was launched, and it now has over 700 members internationally (www.nordp.org/).

NORDP hosts an annual conference that showcases research development best practices. If your institution does not have research development services, several consulting firms will travel to your institution to give one- or two-day workshops or provide hourly proposal writing coaching. Many of these organizations are listed under the Resources tab on the NORDP website: www.nordp.org/resources.

Writing Coaching and Support Groups

If you don't have the willpower to go it alone, mutual shaming accountability can help you adhere to a writing schedule. Look for a writing buddy or join a writing accountability group. Your institution may facilitate annual or summer writing groups, or you can find several excellent sources of writing group support online (some charge fees, some are free), a few of which are listed here:

> The National Center for Faculty Development and Diversity (www.facultydiversity.org/) is a professional development, training, and mentoring community of over 18,000 graduate students, post-docs, and faculty members. They offer several programs to motivate writing consistency and success, including writing workshops and retreats, peer mentoring, accountability buddy matches, monthly writing challenges, and more.
>
> Academic Writing Club (http://academicwritingclub.com/) offers a structured, online coaching system that includes a combination of accountability tools and productivity coaching designed to jumpstart your writing. You work with a supportive online community of experts and colleagues to develop and maintain ideal writing habits.
>
> Summer Academic Working Groups (http://jayandleanne.com/lpowner/pages/sawg/), organized by Leanne Powner, is a forum that allows academics to collaborate electronically for feedback and mutual accountability during the summer. Participants are divided into clusters of four to six individuals in the same academic division who share work in progress on a regular basis and provide each other with feedback.

Writing Success Guides

Boice, R. (1983). Contingency management in writing and the appearance of creative ideas: Implications for the treatment of writing blocks. *Behaviour Research and Therapy, 21*(5), 537–543.

Boice, R. (1990). *Professors as Writers: A Self-Help Guide to Productive Writing.* Stillwater, OK: New Forums Press.

Elbow, P. (1998). *Writing Without Teachers*. New York: Oxford University Press.

Elbow, P. (1998). *Writing With Power: Techniques for Mastering the Writing Process*. New York: Oxford University Press.

Elbow, P. (1989). Toward a phenomenology of freewriting. *Journal of Basic Writing, 8*(2), 42–71.

Silvia, P. J. (2007). *How to Write a Lot: A Practical Guide to Productive Academic Writing*. Washington, DC: American Psychological Association.

BOX 15.1   FLASH TOPIC: FEDERAL FUNDING AGENCIES IN A NUTSHELL

Throughout this book we refer to a variety of federal agencies that support humanities and social science research through grants and fellowships. The following summary includes their names, acronyms, and website links, as well as brief explanations for where to find the appropriate humanities and social science opportunities within each agency.

DOD—Department of Defense www.defense.gov/

- The Minerva Research Initiative: funds social science research that builds deeper understanding of the social, cultural, and political dynamics that shape regions of strategic interest around the world (http://minerva.dtic.mil/).
- Multidisciplinary University Research Initiative Program (MURI): This multidisciplinary funding opportunity serves to stimulate innovations, accelerate research progress, and expedite transition of results into military applications. MURI awards are made in research topics specified by the participating defense agencies each year, which sometimes include topics in social and behavioral sciences. Topics change annually.
  - Army Research Office (ARO): www.arl.army.mil/www/default.cfm?page=29
  - Air Force Office of Scientific Research (AFOSR): www.wpafb.af.mil/afrl/afosr
  - Office of Naval Research (ONR): www.onr.navy.mil/

DOJ—Department of Justice, Office of Justice Programs http://ojp.gov/funding/index.htm

Most social science research funding at DOJ can be found in the Office of Justice Programs. They fund research on criminal and juvenile justice systems and support services.

DOT—Department of Transportation
www.transportation.gov

The Department of Transportation mainly funds university research through their University Transportation Centers (UTC) Program.

ED—Department of Education www.ed.gov/

The Institute of Education Science (IES) supports education and social science research that contributes to school readiness and improved academic achievement, particularly for students whose education prospects are hindered by inadequate education services and conditions associated with poverty, race/ethnicity, limited English proficiency, disability, and family circumstance (https://ies.ed.gov/funding/).

NEA—National Endowment for the Arts www.arts.gov/

The NEA funds two grants for individuals (as opposed to arts organizations), that may be relevant to humanities research:

- Creative writing fellowships
- Translation projects

NEH—National Endowment for the Humanities
www.neh.gov

Multiple grants for humanities research and activities categorized in seven divisions:

- Education Program
- Preservation and Access
- Public Programs
- Research Programs
- Challenge Grants
- Digital Humanities

NIH—National Institutes of Health www.nih.gov/

The Office of Behavioral and Social Sciences Research (OBSSR) coordinates health-relevant behavioral and social sciences at NIH and identifies opportunities to advance these sciences though the work of the NIH's 27 institutes and centers. Funding opportunities led by OBSSR can be found here: https://

obssr.od.nih.gov/. Extramural funding opportunities are divided into four main grant types:

- Research Grants (R series)
- Career Development Awards (K series)
- Research Training and Fellowships (T & F series)
- Program Project/Center Grants (P series)

NOAA—National Oceanic and Atmospheric Administration www.noaa.gov/

NOAA funds climate-related social science research through its Climate Program Office, particularly through the Climate and Societal Interactions (CSI) Program (http://cpo.noaa.gov/ClimatePrograms/ClimateandSocietalInteractions.aspx).

NSF—National Science Foundation www.nsf.gov/

Grants for social science research can be found mainly in two of the foundation's seven academic directorates:

- Social and Behavioral Sciences
- Education and Human Resources

USDA—United States Department of Agriculture www.usda.gov/wps/portal/usda/usdahome

USDA funds food- and agriculture-related social science research through the National Institute for Food and Agriculture (NIFA), https://nifa.usda.gov/. Relevant programs include:

- Agriculture and Food Research Initiative (AFRI)
- Environmental and Resource Economics Programs

16

PARTING WORDS FOR INSTITUTIONS AND INVESTIGATORS

An Epilogue to Institutional Leadership

The data show that nationally, the majority of funding for humanities and social sciences comes from institutions of higher education through mechanisms such as internal grants and new faculty start-up funds (National Science Foundation 2016). Federal funding for the humanities and social sciences has been flat or declining in real dollars, and alarmingly, has been under attack by various lawmakers as well. Both institutional funds and private foundation funding is subject to fluctuations in the state, national, and global economy.

How can colleges and universities support proposal development and research for their humanists and social scientists under these unpredictable conditions?

Don't Compare the Humanities and Social Sciences to STEM Disciplines

It is unrealistic to expect humanists and social scientists to behave like STEM faculty in their patterns of grantsmanship. As the data in this book illustrate, there are simply fewer opportunities, and the amount of funding available is a drop in the bucket compared to that for STEM fields.

Although humanities and social science funding may not add substantially to the bottom line of extramural funds and indirect costs, there are other important benefits to having a vibrant humanities and social science research environment at your institution. Institutional prestige is at stake, and certain measures of humanities and social science vitality, such as awards and honors, may go into rankings and membership thresholds for national associations, such as the Association of American Universities (AAU). How many Guggenheim or MacArthur fellows does your institution have, for instance? The majority of these have traditionally gone to non-STEM scholars. Institutional rankings, by *U.S. News & World Report* or Leiden, for example, are also reliant on a comprehensive assessment of activities at your institution.

The pattern of grantsmanship for individual humanists and social scientists is cyclical. In these disciplines, we are not continuously seeking funds for research, as is often required to support STEM research, laboratories, and students. As emphasized in this book, humanities and social science research is usually conducted alone. As such, there are only so many projects that one can accomplish at a time, and each project may take several years, particularly if it culminates in a book. Thus, it cannot be expected that the majority of humanists and social scientists will apply for multiple grants every year throughout their careers. It is more often the case that we will embark on a grant writing campaign every few years or so to fund the next project. Once that is completed, we start the cycle again.

This pattern and pace, however, are changing as humanists and social scientists become more involved in collaborative and interdisciplinary work. To this end, supporting a strong research environment for us at your institution can improve the options for internal collaborations and the inception of novel and innovative team work *in situ*. Institutional support for interdisciplinary team building in strategic areas can have enormous payoff when opportunities for relevant grants come along.

Research Development for Humanities and Social Science

The profession of research development has exploded since 2009, largely in response to the economic downturn that began in 2008. Colleges and universities recognized that to become or remain competitive in the extramural funding race, faculty and graduate students would need new types of professional development, coaching, and staff support. After forming in 2009 with 39 members, the National Organization of Research Development Professionals (NORDP) counted over 700 members from over 340 institutions in the United States and abroad in 2016 (www.nordp.org/).

However, very few research development professionals are dedicated to the humanities and social sciences. Almost 50% of research development offices are located centrally in institutions, such as in the Office of Research. Another 25% are located at the college or school level. Sixty-four percent of research development offices have four or fewer staff members, and the majority of research development professionals have expertise in STEM fields. It is more common for a Research Development Office to have staff who are expected to provide services to all disciplines on a campus, with most support going towards large grants and STEM fields.

Although it may not always be feasible to hire research development staff who are experienced in, and dedicated to, the non-STEM disciplines, there are important ways that institutions can understand the idiosyncrasies of the humanities and social sciences in order to support them effectively.

Humanists and social scientists can accomplish their research with little or no funding. Given the paltry sums of extramural funding available, there may not be incentives to pursue larger external grants if internal sources of funds are enough to get by on. Faculty members may be asking themselves:

> Why spend months perfecting a proposal to the National Endowment for the Humanities, when there is only a 7% chance of success? Wouldn't that time be better spent on publications? Especially if I will be seen as a failure if I am not successful getting the grant!

This type of conundrum points to a puzzle of incentives and rewards that needs to be disentangled in the context of your institution. Department chairs, deans, and provosts should think through the following set of questions:

- What programs can be developed to reduce the barriers to grantsmanship for humanists and social scientists and reward them for even trying?
- Can grantsmanship be recognized by departmental and higher-level promotion committees as scholarly activity alongside publications?
- Are resources for seed funding, collaboration, course release, and student assistance aligned with institutional expectations or goals for humanities and social science grantsmanship?
- What professional development programs can be implemented to increase humanities and social science proposal development and writing?

Communities of Support

We have seen a particular scenario play out again and again. Many humanists and social scientists apply for fellowships and grants in secret, often even submitting proposals without institutional review, in order to avoid the shame of failure should they not be successful. After trying once or twice unsuccessfully, they give up. There are many ways to change this situation on your campus.

First, foster a grantsmanship culture for graduate students and faculty in which failure is one step on the path to success. Even for great proposals, the first time is not always the charm. Neither is the second or the third in many cases. Department chairs and mentors should reassure students and faculty members new to proposal writing that they will eventually succeed if they do not give up.

Second, provide specialized training for proposal writing. Don't expect humanists and social scientists to get as much out of all-campus proposal writing "boot camps" or workshops. If your campus does not have a Research Development Office, or if the expertise in your Research Development Office is more aligned with STEM fields, you can enlist experienced humanities and social science faculty members to teach workshops or preside over mock review panels. You can also provide modest funding for faculty members to attend funding agency events, such as NSF Days or an NIH Regional Seminar, or visit a program officer at their target agency.

Third, provide infrastructure for communities and team building. Help faculty form proposal writing groups by providing space and food for their meetings. Recognize faculty for winning grants and fellowships by hosting receptions or lunches to honor them publicly. Examine the potential interdisciplinary research strengths at your institution, and develop events to build research teams, such as mini-symposia, colloquia, or retreats.

Advocacy

College presidents, provosts, deans, and department chairs should become involved in various organizations that advocate on behalf of the humanities and social sciences at the state and federal levels. Some key organizations are:

- NHA—National Humanities Alliance: www.nhalliance.org/
- Your state humanities council and the Federation of State Humanities Councils: www.statehumanities.org/
- COSSA—Consortium of Social Science Organizations: www.cossa.org/
- American Association for the Advancement of Science: www.aaas.org/
- Imagining America: http://imaginingamerica.org/

If your institution participates in a large consortium of institutions or a higher education advocacy organization, such as the Association of Public & Land Grant Universities (APLU) or the Association of American Universities (AAU), become involved in their targeted efforts to support and strengthen the humanities and social sciences.

Along with advocating in traditional arenas on behalf of your institution, consider ways to build a stronger public identity for the humanities and social sciences in your own community. Develop new "town and gown" initiatives to engage the public in our important disciplines and the results of our research. Given that state and federal funding for research and higher education is becoming more influenced by voter preferences, help make your neighboring communities more aware of the benefits of humanities and social sciences in their lives.

Encouragement for Students and Faculty

Funding for the humanities and social sciences has become increasingly competitive, with no end to this trend in sight. On top of that, proposal writing is a genre that is different from other forms of academic writing and not taught systematically in most graduate programs. In this challenging environment, this book was written with the goal of demystifying the process and helping faculty and students write the most competitive proposals possible. We also hope that it introduces new approaches to attract funding for humanities and social science research, for example, through collaboration, community-engaged scholarship, and crowdfunding.

For the graduate students and faculty members reading this book, we hope that we have conveyed how exciting and rewarding proposal writing can be. Not only will it lead to awards that fund your research, but proposal writing itself is a fantastic medium in which to unleash your creativity, dreams, and long-term career goals. The process of writing and submitting proposals will give you multiple opportunities to meet and network with like-minded scholars and communicate your research within academia and potentially with the public as well.

We wish you tremendous success!

The End.

Bibliography

National Science Foundation, *National Center for Science and Engineering Statistics, Higher Education Research and Development Survey, FY 2015*, www.nsf.gov/statistics/srvyherd/

INDEX

INDEX OF FUNDING AGENCIES